Revise for History GCSE
School History Project

Nigel Kelly   Judith Kidd

Heinemann Educational Publishers
Halley Court, Jordan Hill, Oxford OX2 8EJ
Part of Harcourt Education

Heinemann is the registered trademark of
Harcourt Education Limited

07   06
12   11

British Library Cataloguing in Publication Data is available from the British Library
on request.

10-digit ISBN: 0 435 10136 6
13-digit ISBN: 978 0 435 10136 7

Typset by Tech Set Ltd, Gateshead, Tyne & Wear
Printed and bound in Great Britain at CPI Bath
Cover design by Threefold Design
Cover photo Wellcome Trust

Acknowledgements

The publishers would like to thank the following for permission to reproduce
photographs and illustrations.

p. 13 Gianni Dagli Orti/Corbis; p. 18 Michael Holford; p. 23 Frank Graham; p. 29 (top)
Bodleian Library; p. 36 (top) Royal Collection (bottom) Fotomas; p. 40 Library of
Congress/Corbis; p. 80 Peter Newark; p. 84 (top) Peter Newark, (bottom) New
York Historical Society; p. 89 Denver Public Library; p. 92 Gilcrease Museum, Tulsa,
Oklahoma; p. 93 Peter Newark; p. 97 Peter Newark; p. 101 Mrs J Maxwell Moran;
p. 110 Peter Newark; p. 117 Solo Syndications; p. 126 Vorwarts, Berlin; p. 131
National Archives/Corbis; p. 139 AKG; p. 144 AKG

Contents

Introduction

What do I study in SHP History?

The SHP GCSE course is one of three History syllabuses studied at GCSE. The others are Modern World History and Social and Economic History. All four examination boards have an SHP syllabus and whichever one you study you will have covered the following:

1 A Development Study

Probably Medicine, but possibly Crime and Punishment.

In this study you will be expected to understand the changes that took place in your chosen study, the pace of change and what caused the changes to occur or made it difficult for the changes to happen.

2 A Depth Study

Probably The American West or Nazi Germany, but possibly Elizabethan England, Britain 1815–51, Britain 1900–50 or South Africa.

In this study you will look at a topic over a shorter period of time (around 50 years) and will be expected to have an in-depth knowledge of the events that took place in that period.

3 Coursework

You will have to do two assignments. These will almost certainly be on Modern World Study and History Around Us, though if you are taking the Edexcel examination there are other alternatives.

What sort of questions will I get?

The examination papers are designed to test four things:

1 Can you recall historical information to organise an answer using relevant facts?

2 Can you describe and explain events, changes and issues in history?

3 Can you explain similarities and differences between sources and comment on their usefulness and reliability?

4 Can you explain how different interpretations of the same event can exist?

All of the examination boards set two examination papers with a number of structured questions. That means that they have parts to them. They are not just essays. Often the questions have some sources to study before you answer the questions.

What is on each paper varies from board to board, so make sure you know exactly what your exam is like. For example, each exam board sets a special exercise to test your ability to understand, analyse and evaluate historical sources and interpretations. But which paper it is on varies!

Here is a summary of the examinations set by each board:

OCR (previously MEG)

Paper 1: 2 hours
Questions on the Development Study (Medicine or Crime and Punishment) and Depth Studies (Germany, American West, Britain 1815–51, Elizabethan England, South Africa).

Paper 2: 1 hour 30 minutes
Source-based questions on Medicine or Crime and Punishment.

SEG

Paper 1: 2 hours
Questions on the Development Study (Medicine only), including a section with source-based questions.

Paper 2: 1 hour 30 minutes
Questions on Depth Studies (Germany, American West, Britain 1815–51, Elizabethan England).

NEAB
Paper 1: 1 hour 30 minutes
Questions on the Development Study (Medicine only).

Paper 2: 2 hours
Questions on Depth Studies (Germany, American West, Britain 1815–51, Elizabethan England), including a section with source-based questions.

Edexcel
Paper 1: 1 hour 45 minutes
Questions on the Development Study (Medicine or Crime and Punishment) and Depth Studies (Germany, American West, Britain 1815–51, Britain 1900–50).

Paper 2: 1 hour 30 minutes
Source-based questions on Medicine or Crime and Punishment.

What is in this revision guide?
We have selected the topics which the vast majority of you study. So the revision guide covers:

1 Development Study: Medicine Through Time.
2 Study in Depth: Nazi Germany and the American West.

In each section you will find:

Topic Summary

Sometimes studying history in depth can be confusing because you get to know so much detail that you lose sight of the 'big picture'. So we start each section with a summary of what the topic is about.

What do I need to know?

The revision guide then gives you the main points that you need to know to answer questions in the examination. Facts are included, but not in the same detail as in your textbook and notes. We are not telling you the whole story again, but instead are summarising it to make it easier for you to learn.

Summary boxes are also included to give you a handy visual summary. When you have completed your revision you should be able to take a summary box and write at length about each point that is shown in it.

What do I know?

Once you have completed your revision you might like to test yourself to see how much you know. We have included a short self-assessment section so that you can see just how thorough your revision has been. Most of the questions can be answered from information given in the summary, but we also presume that you have been learning the information in your book and notes!

Using the Sources

A vital part of any history course is being able to use sources. We have, therefore, put a number of 'using the sources' exercises in the book. Sometimes we give you even more help by adding hints on how to the answer the questions.

Exam Type Questions

You may be studying history because you love it and not care about how you do in the exam. For most students, however, what they really want is to do as well as possible in the examination. So we have given you lots of examples of the types of questions you will be asked together with some student answers.

Examiner's Comments

The authors of this book are experienced SHP Senior Examiners and they have commented on each exam question answer. By reading their comments you will be able to see what is good and what is disappointing in the answer. Then you can make sure that any answer you give in the exam is much better.

Factors and Turning Points in Medicine

One of the annoying things about the examination is that it is not enough to know what happened in medicine. You also have to be able to explain what part certain factors (such as chance) played and whether certain events were important enough to be called 'turning points'. We have included a section on how to do this and some practice questions to make sure you are fully prepared for the examination.

What is the best way to revise?

1 Be organised
You can't revise properly if you don't have all the necessary material. So make sure that your work is in order and up to date.

Keep your file properly organised (why not number the pages in case the file splits open?) and separate essential information (like notes) from useful information (like tests and pieces of homework).

2 Revise regularly
Revision is not something which you should leave until the last few weeks (or days!) before an exam. If you can learn as you go along then it will be much easier to take it all in before the final exam. Try to find a few minutes each week to go over what it is you have studied. If there is anything you haven't fully understood get it cleared up now!

3 Plan a proper revision timetable
The last few months of your course can be a stressful and worrying time. So make a sensible revision timetable and stick to it. Make sure you set yourself realistic targets. You know yourself better than anyone else and you know what it is you can do.

It's no good saying that you will do eight hour's revision on a certain day. You won't be able to do it and then you will get depressed. But you probably could manage four lots of one hour revision slots with a break to do something you enjoy in between each one. This is a much better way to revise anyway, because after an hour your concentration will start to go, so you need a break.

4 Use your guide
If you try to revise by simply reading your work you will soon get bored and you won't take it all in. So read a small section of your file, read our summary text and then make some simple revision notes. Read these through and when you think you know your work try extending the points in the summary boxes. Once you are happy with the topic, answer the 'What do I know?' section and then do the sources and examination question work. By then you should be well prepared.

5 Stay Cool
At examination time everyone is stressed. To do well you not only have to be well-prepared, but you also have to control your own feelings of panic. Stick to your revision timetable and practice answering questions. Then you'll be fine, but make sure you arrive for the examination in plenty of time. You have enough to do without worrying about being late.

6 Be lucky
Lucky people get questions in the examination on the very bits they have revised most thoroughly. Since we can't guarantee that this will happen to you, it's best to revise everything thoroughly. Then you are bound to be lucky!

Here's hoping the revision goes well, the exam goes even better and the results go best of all!

Medicine Through Time

A development study looks at a topic over a long period of time. You will need to know what happened in medicine throughout the period to answer questions like:

What do I need to know in this development study?

- Which area of medicine had most/least change in each period?
- Why did these changes take place?
- What held back medical progress?
- Did change always happen at the same rate?
- Was change always a good thing?
- Who were the most important people in medicine in this period?
- Why were they so important?

Remember that certain aspects of medicine will be examined in each period. These include:

- What *caused* disease and what was done to cure/prevent it?
- Did anyone take action to *prevent* disease?
- What was known about the structure of the body (anatomy)?
- What was known about how the body worked (physiology)?
- How advanced was surgery?
- How advanced was the use of drugs?
- Who treated and looked after the sick?
- What part did the government play in promoting public health?

You will also need to know how far the following factors influenced the development of medicine:

- Government
- Religion
- War
- Individuals
- Science and technology
- Chance
- Teamwork
- Communications.

To help in revising the topic, on the next page is a check list of the periods you have studied and the key aspects of each.

Medicine Through Time – A Summary

Period	Main events/trends	Individuals	Factors
Prehistoric	• Supernatural and common sense medicine		• Nomadic lifestyle
Ancient Egyptian	• Progress in anatomy, surgery, physiology, pharmacy, doctors • Some prevention of disease	• Imphotep – god of healing	• Trade • Slaves (time to think) • Observation • Religion
Ancient Greek	• Development of natural explanations – Four Humours • Clinical observation improves knowledge of diseases • Supernatural ideas continue e.g. Asklepios	• Asklepios – god of healing • Hippocrates	• Trade • Slaves • Philosophy • Interest in natural world
Ancient Roman	• Natural and supernatural ideas continue • Galen (Use of Opposites) treats imbalanced humours • Knowledge of anatomy improved by Galen and dissection (mainly animal) • Public health system across the Empire. Link between dirt and disease	• Asklepios – god of healing • Claudius • Galen	• Need for a strong empire • Taxes • Trade • Engineering skills • Observation • Greek ideas and experience
Medieval (a) Western Europe	• Regression to supernatural explanations – God causes and cures • Catholic Church controls ideas and accepts Galen as expert on the human body • Decline in public health, knowledge and learning as Roman ideas lost to all but a few • Some natural ideas continue, e.g. humours		• Power of Christianity • Loss of Roman knowledge • Wars with Islamic world • Lack of organised government
(b) Islamic world	• Continued interest in medicine – Greek and Roman books studied • Small developments made by individuals • No dissection	• Rhazes • Ibn Sina (Avicenna) • Ibn an Nafis	• Religion • Wars with Christian Europe • Individuals
Renaissance	• Renewed interest in medicine and a new questioning approach • Galen's mistakes exposed by Vesalius (encourages more research) • Paré makes chance discovery of new surgical technique • Great progress in anatomy and physiology	• Vesalius • Paré • Harvey	• Printing • Art • Relaxation of religion, e.g. more dissection • Roman and Greek ideas • Observation and experimentation – science
18th century	• Prevention of smallpox accepted	• Jenner	• Science – observation and testing • Chance
19th century – Industrial Revolution	• Public health crisis in early period – cholera epidemics • Government intervention brings public health reforms • Spontaneous generation disproved by Pasteur and germ theory – turning point for cause and cure and prevention of disease • Vaccinations developed • Progress in surgery with antiseptics and anaesthetics	• Pasteur • Simpson • Lister • Nightingale • Koch • Chadwick	• Industry • Technology • Science • Crimean War • The extension of the vote • Individuals • International rivalry • Communications • Government
20th century	• Two world wars help and hinder medicine • Penicillin and magic bullets revolutionise cures • NHS and welfare state set up • Hi-tech surgery and medicine • New diseases and health debates • Problems with world health	• Ehrlich • Fleming • Domagk • Florey • Chain	• Technology • Science • World Wars I and II • Chance • Communications • Government

Prehistoric Medicine

....1...................................

Topic Summary

The prehistoric period is the starting point in our study but since there is no surviving written evidence we cannot be sure what medicine was like. We can gain clues by looking at physical remains and other similar groups alive today. The best example is the Aborigines. A study of their approach to medicine suggests that prehistoric people had supernatural ideas about disease but also some practical treatments.

....2...................................

What do I Need to Know?

- Prehistoric people led a nomadic lifestyle – they travelled in search of food and followed the animals to survive. They did not settle or farm and therefore had little time to investigate or question the world.
- Prehistoric people believed in spirits and supernatural explanations for events. Every living thing had a spirit and events such as life, death and disease were caused by this spirit.
- Prehistoric people did have simple tools, such as flint arrowheads for spears.
- These tools were used in trephining – the drilling of holes in the skull to release evil spirits. Skulls have been found in which the bone has grown again over the holes, so we know the person had survived.
- Prehistoric people did not write and leave records for future generations. All we have are cave paintings and archaeological remains. So we have to use Australian Aborigines from the beginning of the 20th century to draw some conclusions. They lived in a similar way to prehistoric people.
- Aborigines treated some medical problems in a practical way, such as putting a broken arm in clay, to set the bone.
- They also used spiritual cures, such as a pointing bone to expel evil spirits, crystals, charms and chants. They also used trephining.
- Early Aborigines had a medicine man who had closest contact with the spirits, but also a lot of practical knowledge about herbs and natural treatments, which he might pass on to others in songs and dances.

The chart on page 10 shows how Prehistoric peoples' emphasis on supernatural causes and cures was linked to their lifestyle. However, at the same time they had some practical knowledge and experience which they could use in medicine.

Summary box

Check that you can understand the links between different aspects of Prehistoric life and medicine.

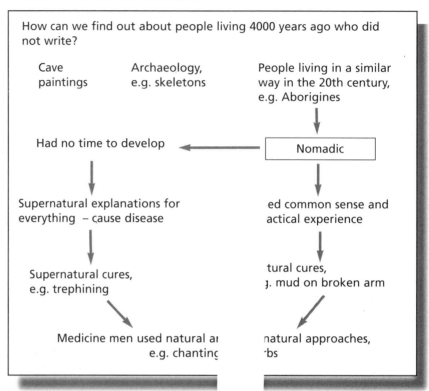

How can we find out about people living 4000 years ago who did not write?

Cave paintings | Archaeology, e.g. skeletons | People living in a similar way in the 20th century, e.g. Aborigines

Had no time to develop ← Nomadic

Supernatural explanations for everything – cause disease

ed common sense and actical experience

Supernatural cures, e.g. trephining

tural cures, ɔ. mud on broken arm

Medicine men used natural aɪ e.g. chantinɡ

natural approaches, ·bs

3

What do I Know?

Once you have revised this topic thoroughly you should be able to answer most of these questions without using your notes. How many can you get right?

1 Give two types of evidence that we can use to find out about Prehistoric people.
2 How do we know what sort of diseases were common in the Prehistoric period?
3 What word do we use to describe groups who do not live a settled lifestyle?
4 What type of anatomy did Prehistoric people have some knowledge of?
5 What was the purpose of trephining?
6 How can we tell that Prehistoric people lived on after they had been trephined?
7 Name two supernatural remedies used by Aborigines.
8 Name two natural remedies used by Aborigines.
9 Give two ways in which medicine men could be seen as early doctors.
10 How did Aborigines pass on knowledge about herbs?

My score……..

Explain why these are important in the development of medicine:

- Prehistoric nomadic lifestyle
- Aborigines in the early 1900s
- Trephining
- Medicine men.

Ancient Egyptian Medicine

The Egyptian period lasted from about 3000 to 400 BC. (Remember that BC dates go backwards!) The key difference between this period and the Prehistoric one is that the Egyptians were not nomadic and their 'civilised' lifestyle gave them time to develop their beliefs and attitudes to religion. Although medicine was still based on religion and illness was thought to be caused by gods, there were the beginnings of natural medicine as some Egyptian doctors prescribed natural cures for patients.

The Egyptians were the first to treat medicine as a profession. Unlike Prehistoric people they were also able to write, so their knowledge could be passed on to future generations.

2
What do I Need to Know?

- The Egyptians were very religious and had many gods and goddesses. These controlled all areas of life, including disease and medicine. Priests communicated with the gods and also used practical treatments. They were often known as doctors.
- A major part of Egyptian belief was that illness was caused by evil spirits entering the body. To cure this the evil spirit had to be driven away.
- Evil spirits could be kept away by wearing charms, such as the scarab beetle. Egyptians also used herbal cures or drugs. They did not think that drugs brought about a natural cure, but instead drove away evil spirits.
- The Egyptians prepared bodies for the return of the soul in the after-life. During embalming they took out the major organs and preserved them. This gave them good knowledge of anatomy and of the use of herbs. But dissection was forbidden, so progress was limited.
- Some Egyptians had the idea that the cause of illness was like the River Nile flooding because its channels became blocked. The body was like this. Its channels got blocked and caused illness. This shows that Egyptians were observant and accepted some natural explanations. This led to some practical cures, such as vomiting and purging, as well as spiritual ones.
- The Egyptians also believed in personal cleanliness. They had some toilets, though no drainage system to carry away the waste.

Summary box

How Medicine Developed in Ancient Egypt

Civilised and settled society ——————→ **Time to develop ideas about religion and medicine**

Egypt – a deeply religious society

Egypt – a practical society

↓

Cleanliness – reduces illness

Observation of the Nile led to new and natural ideas about blocked channels

Embalming – provides knowledge of anatomy, skills in surgery and pharmacy

↓

Natural treatments (purging, bleeding, vomiting)

Respect for doctors – because of link between religion and medicine – gods cause and cure disease

Use of herbs and drugs

Knowledge of anatomy (from embalming) leads to some surgery

But

But

As a body was needed for after-life dissection was not allowed

Most doctors still thought that herbs and drugs drove away evil spirits

This diagram should remind you that like the Prehistoric times the Egyptian period had both natural and supernatural aspects to medicine. Egyptian religion and Egyptian medicine had both become far more complex and progress had been made.

3

What do I Know?

Once you have revised this topic thoroughly you should be able to answer most of these questions without using your notes. How many can you get right?

Explain why these are important in the development of medicine:

- Embalming
- The River Nile
- Scarab beetle charms
- Egyptian writing/ hieroglyphics.

1 Which Egyptian god of war caused and cured epidemics?
2 Which Egyptian god of healing was probably doctor to the Pharoahs?
3 What was new about the idea of blocked channels?
4 Which two treatments started as a result of this idea?
5 How did the Egyptians know about new herbs and spices?
6 Why did embalming help medical progress?
7 Why did belief in the after-life hinder medical progress?
8 Why did Egyptian priests shave themselves daily?
9 Which charm was worn to ward off evil spirits?
10 How did the Egyptians prevent malaria?

My score.........

4

Using the Sources

In your exam you will asked to look at sources and use them to explain developments in medicine. Here are two sources.

Source A

▲ **An Egyptian charm shaped like a beetle**.

Source B

'When you come across a swelling that has attacked a vessel, then it has formed a tumour in your body. If, when you examine it with your fingers, it is hard like a stone, then you should say "It is a tumour of the vessels. I shall treat the disease with a knife".'

▲ **An account written on papyrus in Egyptian times.**

1 Can you explain why the Egyptians wore charms like that in Source A and what this tells us about their medical beliefs?

2 What can you learn about Egyptian medicine from:
   (a) What Source B says.
   (b) The fact that it exists at all?

3 How is the medical idea in Source B different to that shown in Source A?

5

Exam Type Questions

Here is the sort of question that you might find on your exam paper. See how it has been answered and assessed before you answer it yourself.

> Why had progress been made in knowledge about the body between the Prehistoric and Egyptian periods?. Explain your answer using Sources A and B and your knowledge. (**7 marks**)

Source A

▲ **Cave painting from El Pindal, Spain.**

Source B

> Forty-six vessels go from the heart to every limb … There are four vessels to the liver; it is they which give it fluid and air, which afterwards cause all diseases to arise in it by overfilling with blood.

▲ **Ebers Papyrus, Ancient Egypt.**

Answer

Source A shows a cave painting of a mammoth showing its heart. Prehistoric people must have known that animals had hearts. Source B describes different parts of the body and the system of channels in the body. The Egyptians thought that if your channels were blocked then you would be ill. This was a natural idea. They got this idea from the River Nile.

Examiner's Comments on Answer

This student clearly understands the sources and has used some knowledge, but has failed to answer the question apart from a short last sentence. I would give this answer about 2 marks out of 7. This answer mentions what the Egyptians had done, but why had this progress taken place? There is nothing about knowledge of anatomy from embalming, for example. The student has mentioned natural ideas about the working of the body from observation of blocked channels in the River Nile, but not explained it. What about Source A? Why didn't Prehistoric people have much knowledge about the human body (only animals)? Here you would need to explain about how being nomadic gave them little time to investigate medicine, unlike the Egyptians who were a settled civilisation.

Ancient Greek Medicine

The Greeks built a large empire and traded around the Mediterranean, picking up new ideas. This empire lasted from about 800 to 400 BC. The Greeks were civilised like the Egyptians. They also had slaves and therefore time on their hands to develop their ideas and skills. They still believed in the influence of gods and goddesses but also began to have new ideas about the world which were more natural. The most important area of progress in medicine was the new natural explanation for disease that Hippocrates developed, called the Theory of the Four Humours. He also made improvements in observing patients and diagnosing different diseases.

2

What do I Need to Know?

Supernatural causes and cures

- Like the Egyptians, the Greeks believed that gods and goddesses caused most things to happen. They explained nature through stories of the actions of these gods. For example, the seasons changed because Demeter was so angry that her daughter Persephone was trapped in Hades for half of each year that she would not allow the plants to grow until she was released.
- Asklepios was the Greek god of healing. His temples were called 'Asklepions' and people went there to be cured. He had several daughters, one of whom was called Hygiea. She helped care for the sick people in his temple. From her name we get the word 'hygienic'. While the sick were in the Asklepion they would bathe themselves, make a gift to the gods, and rest. People believed that they were cured by Asklepios, visiting them in the night.
- The cured often made inscriptions in the stone walls describing the success of their cures.
- Temples of Asklepion were also very healthy places. They had baths, arenas and abatons, which were open-air buildings.

Spread of ideas

- Like the Romans, the Greeks had an empire. Their land was split up into independent city-states who traded with each other and across the Mediterranean. This way they spread their ideas and picked up others.
- The Greeks were also great thinkers. Education developed and a new thinking called philosophy ('love of wisdom') was practised. This involved asking questions and looking for natural explanations for every event.

Natural explanations and Hippocrates

- The most important example of Greek natural thinking is the work of Hippocrates. He developed the first widespread natural explanation for disease involving four humours in the body, which had to be balanced.
- The four humours were also connected to the seasons when certain illnesses were more common. For example, people were more likely to have an imbalance of phlegm in the winter months and this meant you would become ill.
- Hippocrates believed in 'clinical observation', where the doctor must observe the patient carefully in order to recognise the illness and suggest an appropriate treatment. This way doctors got to learn a lot about the courses different diseases take and their symptoms. Hippocrates and his followers described different diseases in the 'Hippocratic Collection'.
- Hippocrates also wrote a book called *A Programme of Health* in which he encouraged personal hygiene and exercise in order to prevent disease.

Summary box

Check that you understand and can explain the links shown in the summary chart.

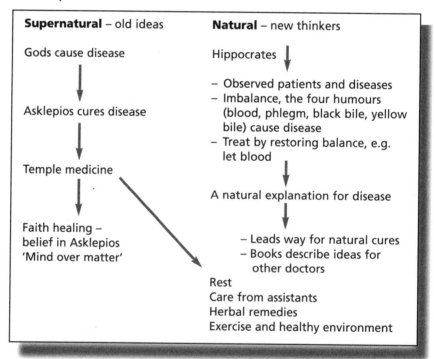

This diagram reminds us that there were two aspects to Greek medicine and that natural ideas did not suddenly replace supernatural ones. Both natural and supernatural methods could be used at the same time. If your local doctor failed, you visited a temple of Asklepios. Although 'Temple Medicine' was supernatural it did bring some progress to medicine in the care that patients were given and the emphasis on a healthy and hygienic environment.

······3············

What do I Know?

Once you have revised this topic thoroughly you should be able to answer most of these questions without using your notes. How many can you get right?

1 List the four humours.
2 How did the idea of the four humours connect to the seasons?
3 What had to be the state of the four humours for a person to be in good health?
4 Name two practical treatments connected to the four humours.
5 Give two ways in which Asklepios' supernatural healing also led to progress in medicine.
6 The Greeks traded with many countries around the Mediterranean. Name two benefits of this for medicine.
7 What did clinical observation involve?
8 Name the books in which Hippocrates' ideas were recorded.
9 Give one piece of advice from Hippocrates' *Programme of Health*.
10 Why was Hippocrates' idea about the four humours wrong? Give two reasons why his mistake was very useful in the history of medicine.

My score………

Explain why these are important in the development of medicine:

- New thinking called philosophy
- The Hippocratic Collection (60 medical books)
- Clinical observation
- The four humours
- Temple medicine

When you think about why people/ideas are important remember to think long term as well as short term, i.e. what did they lead to in the future.

How did Greek ideas lead the way to:
- Galen and the Use of Opposites
- Bloodletting as a treatment
- Increased health and hygiene?

······4·····················

Using the Sources

Study Sources A and B. What can these sources tell us about Greek attitudes to healing?

Source A

Aegestratos was unable to sleep because of headaches. As soon as he came to the temple he fell asleep and had a dream. He thought that the god cured him of his headache and, making him stand up, taught him wrestling. The next day he departed cured, and after a short time he competed at the Nemean games, and was victor in the wrestling.

▲ **Carved on a stone tablet found at a Temple of Asklepios.**

Source B

▲ Carving on the tombstone of Jason, a doctor from Athens. It shows Jason, his patient, and a bleeding cup.

Here are some ideas about how to answer this question, using your knowledge of the history of medicine and Sources A and B. Don't panic! Look at the sources. Ask yourself these questions.

- What do I recognise in the writing/picture (what words/ideas)?
- What is going on in the source?
- What is the message of the source?
- What does it tell me about medicine at the time?
- Is it a typical source for this time? Where does it come from? Can we trust it?
- What else do I know that helps me to make sense of this evidence?

Now apply these questions to these two sources – a written one and a picture. You can use these questions to help you with most sources in this study. Make notes for each question and turn the notes into a written answer to the overall question.

Ancient Roman Medicine

After 500 BC the Romans began to build a large empire in Europe. They used many Greek ideas about medicine and took some of them a step further. The main idea they developed was that of a public health system – not just a few sewers in Rome but a whole network of facilities across their empire.

Although Romans still believed in gods and goddesses their doctors continued to work on natural ideas. Galen, for example, developed treatments for the four humours called the Use of Opposites. He was a famous doctor and worked for the Roman emperor. Galen's main contribution, however, was in the study of anatomy. He built up a much more detailed picture of the human body by dissection, but he did make some mistakes.

2

What do I Need to Know?

Faith healing

- Like the Greeks, the Romans had both natural and supernatural explanations for illness. They shared many of the Greek ideas about gods and goddesses, although they gave them different names.
- They worshipped the same god of healing as the Greeks – Asklepios – and continued to build temples of Asklepios where 'Temple Medicine' was practised.

Galen and Use of Opposites

- Claudius Galen was the key medical man in the Roman period. He was Greek and had trained as a doctor at the Asklepion in Pergamum. He developed treatments called the Use of Opposites which were linked to Hippocrates' four humours. He treated people with the opposite of their ailment. For example, for a cold he might prescribe a hot bath and pepper.
- His main area of work was anatomy and physiology. He observed some human skeletons at medical school in Alexandria, but mainly had to rely on dissecting animals because human dissection was forbidden. He learnt a lot about the structure of the body and how it worked. He wrote down his findings in over 100 books, which became the basis for medical teaching for 1,500 years.

Public health

- The Roman public health system was the key area of progress in this period. It was very extensive. The Romans built sewers, aqueducts, water fountains, public baths, lead water pipes and public toilets, all over the empire.

- There was a need for a public health system in Rome as it grew into an overcrowded city. But the Romans also wanted a healthy empire and especially healthy soldiers to protect the empire.
- Having such a large and organised empire was very important for the Romans' success. For example, taxing their subjects made them rich. They also had slaves for manpower.
- Although the Romans did not know about germs their observations told them that disease might be caused by several things. These included sewage, bad air and dirty water. Clean water was very important to the Romans.

Summary box 1

Galen's Influence on Medicine		
Area of medicine	**Positive (helping)**	**Negative (hindering)**
Anatomy and physiology	• Knowledge about the body, e.g. brain controls body through nerves • His ideas fitted in with religions • Wrote his ideas down for others to learn	• Made mistakes – dissected animals, e.g. structure of the jaw bone • Ideas fitted with religions • No one dared criticise him as this would reflect on the Church
Surgery	• Worked with gladiators in Pergamum – got knowledge of anatomy	
Doctors as professionals	• Worked for the emperor in Rome. Became famous • Used Hippocrates' high standards of patient care and observation	• Perhaps his reputation was another reason why no one dared to challenge him
Treatments	• The Use of Opposites encouraged natural treatments • Was developing the work of Hippocrates, so was accepted	

This chart should remind you of the ways in which Galen helped medicine, but also how he may have held back some progress. Can you add any other points to the chart?

Here is a list of possible factors that helped Galen to make progress in anatomy and physiology.

- Religion allowed dissection, but mainly on animals
- Some human dissection was allowed at Alexandria
- Galen's reputation
- His background and training.

Tasks

- What do you know about each factor?
- Explain how each one helped him – or, if appropriate, how it hindered medieval progress.

Summary box 2

Rome crowded and smelly River Tiber polluted

Emperor and officials want decent conditions

People enjoyed a visit to the baths

A strong army

Taxes from the empire

Architects and engineers

Need for a healthy army

Desire to spread proof of superiority of Roman ideas

Knew about a link between dirt and disease (not germs)

Roman public health

Spread across the empire
How long did it last?

The Romans had: baths, aqueducts, cisterns, public toilets, water fountains
What else?

Tasks

- Check that you understand and can give details and explanations to each factor which led to Roman public health.
- Which of the factors do you think are the most important?
- Are any connected – if so, how?
- Did the rich Roman citizens benefit more than the poor?

Summary box 3

The Romans did not just come up with all their own new ideas. They were influenced by civilisations and places they conquered as part of their empire. They also spread their ideas as they expanded. Check that you understand and can explain these links in the spread of ideas:

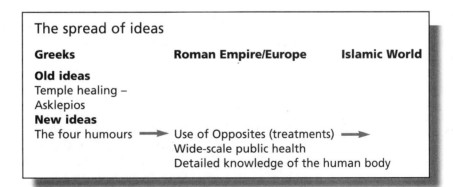

The spread of ideas

Greeks	**Roman Empire/Europe**	**Islamic World**
Old ideas		
Temple healing – Asklepios		
New ideas		
The four humours ⟶	Use of Opposites (treatments) ⟶	
	Wide-scale public health	
	Detailed knowledge of the human body	

This diagram should remind you that both Greeks and Romans had natural and supernatural causes and cures for disease.

3

Influences of the East

Remember that it was not only the Egyptians, Greeks and Romans who made progress in medicine. Ideas from China and India spread elsewhere and influenced medicine. As in the Western world, Eastern medicine included both natural and supernatural ideas. Yin and Yang, for example, was a system of the balance of two energies in the body. The Chinese also carried out acupuncture to help unblock invisible channels in the body. We did not know as much about these ideas for many years because of poor communications. China, for example, was isolated from the rest of the world and distracted by wars between different states. But some ideas managed to reach the West along the silk trade route by way of India.

Summary box 4

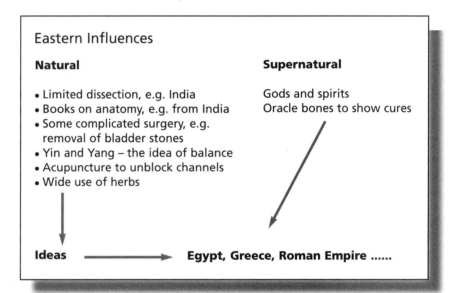

Eastern Influences

Natural

- Limited dissection, e.g. India
- Books on anatomy, e.g. from India
- Some complicated surgery, e.g. removal of bladder stones
- Yin and Yang – the idea of balance
- Acupuncture to unblock channels
- Wide use of herbs

Supernatural

Gods and spirits
Oracle bones to show cures

Ideas ⟶ **Egypt, Greece, Roman Empire ......**

This summary should remind you that Eastern medicine included natural and supernatural ideas, as well as medicine in the Western world. There seem to be similarities between Chinese medicine and the ideas from Egypt and the Greeks. Their lifestyles and environments were similar – they were all civilised societies which had time to develop theories and observe more about the human body.

Tasks

- Make a list of similarities between Eastern medicine and the ideas in Ancient Egypt, Greece and Rome.
- Which Greek idea is similar to Yin and Yang in that it is based on the idea of balance?
- Which other civilisation believed in unblocking channels in the body to restore health?

4   What do I Know?

Once you have revised this topic thoroughly you should be able to answer most of these questions without using your notes. How many can you get right?

Explain why these are important in the development of medicine:

- The Roman god of healing
- Galen
- The Roman army
- Indian medical books describing dissections
- Chinese idea of Yin and Yang.

How did Roman ideas lead the way to:

- Ibn an Nafis
- Vesalius?

1 Give three different kinds of medical work done by Galen.

2 List two aspects of anatomy that Galen got wrong.

3 What was the short-term reason for his mistakes?

4 What was the background reason for his mistakes?

5 Give an example of a treatment that follows Galen's theory about the Use of Opposites.

6 Make a list of three types of building/engineering that were part of the Roman public health system.

7 Give two main reasons why the Romans had a public health system.

8 Which Greek ideas did the Romans develop most?

9 How did the Indians get their knowledge of anatomy?

10 What natural explanation of disease was developed by the Chinese before Hippocrates' Four Humours?

My score........

5   Using the Source

Look at this artist's reconstruction of a toilet at Hadrian's Wall and answer the question below.

What does this source tell us about Roman public health? How reliable do you think this impression is? (See next page for some hints.)

Hints for your answer

- Use your knowledge to explain what is going on in the source.
- Think what the source is about. Hadrian's Wall was a base for the army so this source may only tell us about the facilities that the army had.
- Think about how accurate the artist's impression might be.
- If you get stuck use the questions on page 16 to help you.

6

Exam Type Question

Here is the sort of question that you might find on your exam paper. See how it has been answered and assessed before you answer it yourself.

> The Romans just copied the Greek ideas about the cause and cure of disease. Do you agree? Use Sources A and B and your knowledge in your answer. **(8 marks)**

Source A

> When all these humours are truly balanced a person feels the most perfect health. Illness happens when there is too much or too little or it is entirely thrown out of the body.

▲ **From the writings of Hippocrates, in Ancient Greece.**

Source B

> Give them food which reduces heat, like soup of yellow lentils and minced meat. Their drink should be cooled with ice.

▲ **A treatment based on the work of Roman doctors.**

Answer A

Source B is the same as Source A in that it is describing the four humours - black bile, yellow bile, blood and phlegm - which they thought caused disease. They thought that if one of the humours was out of balance then you would get ill. The Romans did copy the Greek ideas because they used this idea to treat people, like in Source B where it talks about cooling with ice. They also copied Asklepios, the Greek god of healing.

Answer B

The Romans invaded parts of Greece and so were influenced by their ideas. They adopted many of their gods and goddesses, although usually changed their names. They also believed in the four humours (blood, phlegm, yellow bile and black bile) which was developed by the Greek doctor Hippocrates. Source A shows how they believed that the humours had to be balanced for a person to be healthy. They also treated them to restore the balance of the humours. However, the Romans did not just copy all the Greek ideas about the cause and cure of disease. They developed some of their own ideas and Galen, in particular, took Hippocrates' work further.

Examiner's Comments on Answer A

This answer understands the idea of the four humours and uses knowledge to explain how the system worked. Knowledge is also used in the mention of Asklepios being the god of healing for both civilisations, as this information is not from the sources. This answer also refers to both sources but has missed the idea of Source B that is actually different to Source A, in that it is developing a system of different treatments linked to the four humours. Therefore this answer only partly answers the question and I would probably give it 4 marks out of 8.

Examiner's Comments on Answer B

This answer has explained some of the similarities between the Greeks and the Romans using knowledge and the sources. The answer has also understood the differences between Sources A and B, and that the Romans did not just copy the Greeks. Unfortunately the answer has only just mentioned the difference at the end and has not explained it or demonstrated any knowledge. The main difference between Source A and B is that in B Galan has carried on with Hippocrates' work by developing the Use of Opposites theory. This is where a woman with a cold would be treated with a hot remedy like pepper. If this answer had gone on to explain about this idea and how it was a step forward from the Greeks, then it would have got a much higher mark. I would give it about 5 marks out of 8.

Medieval Medicine – Western Europe

.... 1 ....

Topic Summary

After the collapse of the Roman Empire much of Western Europe no longer had strong government. There were many wars and a breakdown in communications between countries. The Catholic Church was very powerful in the period 500–1500 AD. Many people believed that God caused disease. Cures of disease were therefore also supernatural – if God caused disease then there would be nothing practical that you could do about it.

It was not only the causes and cures of disease that regressed in the Middle Ages. Public health and medical learning were also limited. Some governments were not organised and did not see the importance of hygiene. Education was often restricted to monks and natural ideas were not encouraged as these would be against God and the Church. Knowledge from Roman and Greek times was lost to all but a few.

.... 2 ....

What do I Need to Know?

Religion and medicine

- The Middle Ages or Medieval period was highly religious and superstitious. It was thought God caused disease and therefore only he could cure you. In order to do this you could pray, take a specially blessed potion, go on a pilgrimage, or even flagellate (whip) yourself as punishment for your sins.
- In Western Europe the Catholic Church was very powerful. It controlled ideas and did not encourage learning. The work of Galen was accepted as his ideas did not rule out a God, but no one could criticise him and very few even studied him in detail.
- Monarchs were believed to be sent by God and therefore had power from him. Until the 17th century people would queue to be touched by the monarch, who could supposedly cure them of scrofula, or the 'King's evil'.
- Dissection was not accepted as it would prevent the person going to heaven. So progress in anatomy, physiology and surgery was limited.
- The emphasis on supernatural explanations did not mean that there were no natural treatments. Some fitted in with God's complex world, and blood letting, testing urine samples and the use of herbs were popular.

Public health

- In many countries there was no strong central government to organise public health systems, not even clean water. The Roman facilities, such as roads, sewers and aqueducts, fell into disrepair.

- An exception to the dreadful public health situation was the monasteries. They were kept clean to please God. The monasteries helped medicine by developing water systems, studying the books of the Greeks and Romans, and caring for the poor. However monks were usually cut off from the outside world and so people did not learn from their example.
- Sometimes town councils did take action, for example during the Black Death in London in 1347–9 emergency measures were introduced, such as a law to clean the streets. But most people believed the Black Death was caused by God, or the planets, or just bad air. So they tried everything they could to cure it. Action included using herbal mixtures to whipping themselves and avoiding strangers, as well as cleaning the streets.

Surgery

- Surgery in the Middle Ages was simple and external, such as removing cataracts. It was usually carried out by barber-surgeons rather than trained doctors, who thought it beneath them. Hugh and Theodoric of Lucca developed the treatment of wounds by using wine as a cleaning agent or antiseptic, but the idea was not widely adopted.

Summary box 1

This is a summary of the causes and cures of disease in the Middle Ages. Check that you understand and can explain the links between them.

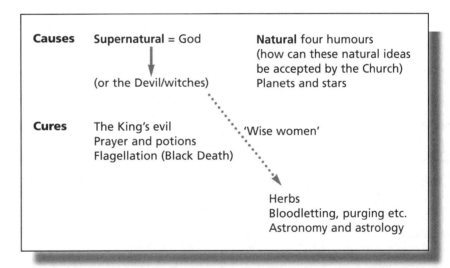

This diagram shows that although supernatural ideas in the Middle Ages were very strong the ideas of the Greeks and Romans were not completely forgotten. No new ideas were developed however, as the Church controlled learning and accepted Galen as the authority on medicine. How does witchcraft show a link between natural and supernatural ideas in the Middle Ages?

Summary box 2

This diagram summarises how medical progress stopped after the collapse of the Roman Empire. Check that you can understand and explain the links.

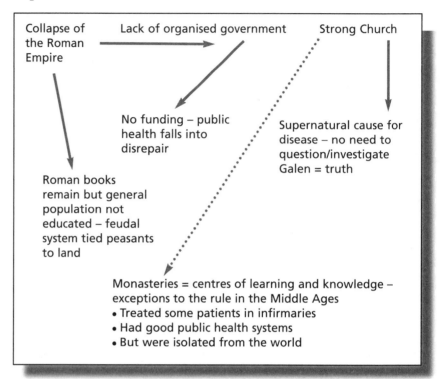

Collapse of the Roman Empire

Lack of organised government

Strong Church

No funding – public health falls into disrepair

Supernatural cause for disease – no need to question/investigate Galen = truth

Roman books remain but general population not educated – feudal system tied peasants to land

Monasteries = centres of learning and knowledge – exceptions to the rule in the Middle Ages
• Treated some patients in infirmaries
• Had good public health systems
• But were isolated from the world

3

What do I Know?

Once you have revised this topic thoroughly you should be able to answer most of these questions without using your notes. How many can you get right?

Explain why these are important in the development of medicine:

- Lack of strong central government
- Monasteries
- The Divine Right of Kings (the belief that they were sent by God)
- The Church's belief in Galen (who explained that the body was created by one God).

1 Why was scrofula known as the 'King's evil'?
2 Why did monarchs believe that they had healing powers?
3 Give two reasons why Christianity in the Middle Ages hindered medicine.
4 Give two reasons why medieval monasteries helped medical progress.
5 Why didn't medieval doctors realise that Galen was sometimes wrong?
6 Give two different things that medieval people believed caused the Black Death.
7 Give two different things they did to cure it.
8 What did people do to try to prevent the plague?
9 What did Hugh and Theodoric of Lucca use to clean wounds?
10 Why was this a good idea?

My score........

Using the Sources

Source A

Look at these two sources from the Middle Ages. They are both showing cures of disease.

▲ Chart for urine testing.

Source B

▲ The King cures scrofula.

> Which of these sources has most in common with the stone carving of a man being bled on page 18?

Hints for your answer

Remember to use your knowledge to explain what is going on in both sources rather than just describe the source that you think is closest to the Greek source. As you explain Sources A and B compare both of them to Source B on page 18.

Medieval Medicine – the Islamic World

1

Topic Summary

Unlike religion in Western Europe the religion of Islam did not hold back medical progress. Individual doctors, such as Rhazes, made some progress in medicine. Islamic countries continued to study Greek and Roman books and kept medicine alive. They also encouraged care for the sick and built hospitals. Religious wars with the West meant that many Ancient ideas and new developments were kept mainly within the Islamic world.

2

What do I Need to Know?

- Developments in knowledge and understanding of diseases took place. Avicenna (or Ibn Sina) wrote a book called the *Canon of Medicine* which was translated into Latin and so spread to Western Europe. Rhazes spotted the difference between smallpox and measles. He was continuing the work of Hippocrates and realised the importance of clinical observation in helping patients and medical knowledge. These developments suggest that medicine was not at a complete standstill in this period.

- Islamic culture and the holy book, the Koran, also encouraged the study of medicine. Many Greek and Roman texts were translated into Arabic and Hippocrates and Galen were highly respected. This kept Ancient ideas alive but did not encourage any criticism.

- Studying and translation of Ancient books meant that some ideas were taken further, for example the ideas of Ibn an Nafis who disproved Galen on the movement of the blood through the septum. This discovery might have been a major turning point, except no one in Europe knew about it until the 20th century.

- Arabs were encouraged by their religion to care for the sick. Hospitals were built in most cities, with trained and licensed doctors. There were separate wards for different diseases and high standards of hygiene.

- Operations were carried out, even the removal of bladder stones, so surgical knowledge had not completely died out. However, dissection was forbidden by Islamic law, and so improvement in anatomy, physiology and surgery was limited.

- One area that did develop was pharmacy. Alchemists developed new apparatus to purify chemicals and extended the use of different drugs, such as laudanum, in medicine.

Summary box 1

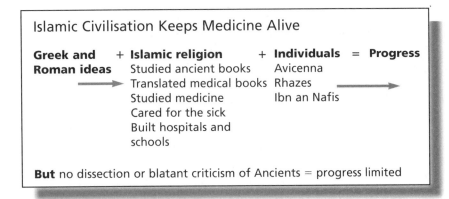

Islamic Civilisation Keeps Medicine Alive

Greek and + **Islamic religion** + **Individuals** = **Progress**
Roman ideas Studied ancient books Avicenna
Translated medical books Rhazes
Studied medicine Ibn an Nafis
Cared for the sick
Built hospitals and
schools

But no dissection or blatant criticism of Ancients = progress limited

This diagram shows that Islamic religion helped keep medicine alive in the East far more than Christianity did in Medieval Europe. Individual examples of progress in medical knowledge were made, but this was also limited. A ban on dissection and high respect for the work of Ancient doctors held back new ideas.

Summary box 2

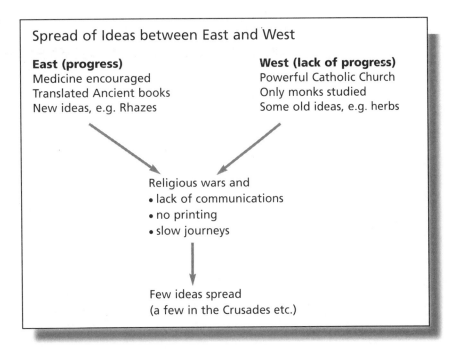

Spread of Ideas between East and West

East (progress) **West (lack of progress)**
Medicine encouraged Powerful Catholic Church
Translated Ancient books Only monks studied
New ideas, e.g. Rhazes Some old ideas, e.g. herbs

Religious wars and
• lack of communications
• no printing
• slow journeys

Few ideas spread
(a few in the Crusades etc.)

This diagram shows that the lack of communication between East and West in the Middle Ages hindered medicine. Although Islamic doctors and scholars studied and translated the work of the Ancient Greeks and Romans little of this knowledge travelled to the West. Although religious wars caused most of this lack of communication they were also an opportunity for contact and some ideas were spread.

.........3.........

What do I Know?

Once you have revised this topic thoroughly you should be able to answer most of these questions without using your notes. How many can you get right?

---

1 Where was the capital of the Islamic Empire?
2 What exactly did Avicenna contribute to the development of medicine?
3 Which two diseases did Rhazes study?
4 Which of Galen's theories did Ibn an Nafis disprove?
5 Why wasn't Ibn an Nafis's work a huge turning point in physiology?
6 What were 'alchemists'?
7 Give an example of an operation that was carried out by Islamic surgeons.
8 Give two reasons why medicine was more advanced in the Islamic world than in the Christian one.
9 Why didn't the Islamic doctors carry out much dissection?
10 Islam and Christianity did have some similar attitudes to medicine in the Middle Ages. Name two ideas they had in common.

My score........

Explain why these are important in the development of medicine:

• The Islamic attitude to the study of Ancient writers
• Ibn an Nafis
• The Crusades.

The Renaissance

....1....

Topic Summary

The word 'Renaissance' means 're-birth', which sums up the approach in this period, the 16th and 17th centuries. Ideas from the Ancient Greeks and Romans were studied once again and improvements were made. Great institutions were criticised, such as the Catholic Church, with the rise of Protestantism (the Reformation). This led to people challenging old ideas and asking questions to find out more. Perhaps Galen could now be studied more critically. Inventions, such as the printing press, helped to spread new ideas across Europe. Most progress was made in anatomy and physiology as religion relaxed and dissection became more acceptable. Progress was also made in surgery.

....2....

What do I Need to Know?

- 'Re-birth' not only happened in medicine. Careful observation led to more accurate art, with artists such as Leonardo da Vinci making detailed anatomical drawings. These helped to spread knowledge about the body as the drawings were printed in books.

- Andreas Vesalius dared prove Galen wrong on several points. He dissected human bodies and challenged Galen's ideas. He said that there were no holes in the septum for blood to pass through. This raised the possibility that Galen could be wrong on other things and that centuries of limited progress in anatomy and physiology could be over.

- Inventions, such as the microscope, were made. Technology also inspired men to understand the human body more. William Harvey discovered that the heart worked like a pump to make blood flow through the body. He worked out this from Vesalius's discovery that blood cannot flow through the holes in the septum. The printing press was another important invention, and this helped to spread detailed information about the human body across Europe.

- In England, Charles II was interested in science and founded the Royal Society in 1661. Many great medical scientists became members and shared ideas. Experimentation and new approaches were encouraged.

- Ambroise Paré developed surgery by challenging old ideas and methods. Sometimes discoveries were made by chance. In Paré's case he stopped using boiling oil on wounds partly because he ran out of oil. Instead he used a natural lotion and bandages which caused less pain and healed wounds more effectively.

Summary box 1

More Medical Knowledge – So What?		
	Andreas Vesalius	**William Harvey**
Discovery/ advance	• Dissected humans • Recorded observations and made detailed illustrations in *The Fabric of the Human Body* (1543) • Dared to point out mistakes that Galen made • Proved Galen wrong about structure of hip and jaw bones, and blood cannot pass through the septum in the heart	• Experimented and measured blood in body • Showed how the blood moves in a one-way system and circulates • Proved that the heart acts like a pump and blood is not burnt up (1616) • Shared ideas in book *On the Motion of the Heart* (1628)
Effects	• Perhaps Galen and other great doctors could be wrong on other medical issues • Encouraged dissection and careful observation • More accurate knowledge of the body • Led to new discoveries, e.g. Harvey	• Explained how Galen was wrong • Showed the importance of scientific method, tests and proof

This diagram reminds you of the main developments made by Vesalius and Harvey, and of the further impact of their work.

Summary box 2

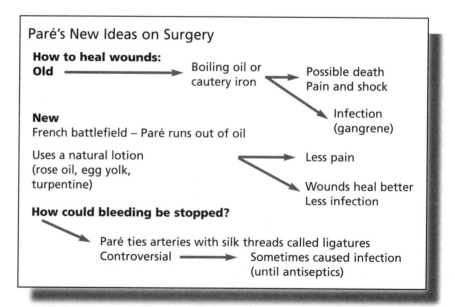

Paré's New Ideas on Surgery

How to heal wounds:
Old → Boiling oil or cautery iron → Possible death / Pain and shock → Infection (gangrene)

New
French battlefield – Paré runs out of oil

Uses a natural lotion (rose oil, egg yolk, turpentine) → Less pain / Wounds heal better Less infection

How could bleeding be stopped?
Paré ties arteries with silk threads called ligatures
Controversial → Sometimes caused infection (until antiseptics)

This diagram shows that Paré was a risk-taker and wanted to improve surgery. He challenged old ideas and proved that his new ones were better for the patient.

Summary box 3

There are many reasons why the Renaissance was a period of so much progress in medicine. Here is a list of factors that contributed to that progress.

Factor of change	Development in medicine
Art	• Vesalius disproves Galen
Technology	• Vesalius' ideas spread across Europe
Communications	• Paré introduces new surgical skills
Less religion	• Harvey works out that blood circulates
More dissection	
Individual determination	
Chance	
Science	

Tasks

- Link up the factors to each medical development.
- Make a list of key words and facts for each point.
- Check that you can explain how they led to change.

What do I Know?

Once you have revised this topic thoroughly you should be able to answer most of these questions without using your notes. How many can you get right?

1. Which were the names of the books that Vesalius, Harvey and Paré wrote to spread their new ideas.
2. Where did Vesalius go to find some of his corpses for dissection?
3. Which famous artist drew detailed drawings of the human anatomy?
4. Who did Harvey work for?
5. Why didn't Harvey's work help to improve operations at the time?
6. What sort of wounds was Paré treating?
7. What three main products made up Paré's lotion?
8. What factors contributed to Pare's success? Which were most important?
9. Why did some people oppose both Vesalius and Harvey?
10. What areas of medicine did not develop much in the Renaissance period?

My score........

Explain why these are important in the development of medicine:

- Leonardo da Vinci
- Padua
- Paré's character.

How did discoveries made by Vesalius, Harvey and Paré eventually help to lead to:

- Fewer deaths from war wounds and accidents
- Successful blood transfusions
- Organ transplants?

4

Using the Sources

Look at these sources. They show two factors of change: the work of artists and technology such as the water pump. Explain how each factor helped progress in medicine during the Renaissance.

Source A

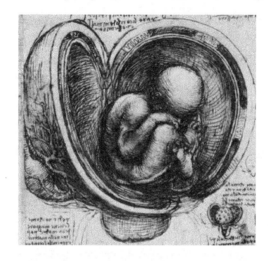

◀ Leonardo da Vinci's drawing of a foetus.

Source B

◀ A water pump.

Hints for your answers

- Use your knowledge to explain each factor.
- Say exactly which area of medicine each factor helped, e.g. anatomy.
- Give an example of an individual or development that was helped by each factor and say how.

5

Exam Type Questions

Here are two questions that might appear in your exam paper.

During the Renaissance Vesalius and Harvey helped bring about progresss in medicine. Choose one of these two people and

1 Describe briefly the main features of his work. **(5 marks)**

2 Could his contribution to medicine have been made before the Renaissance? **(10 marks)**

Question 1: Answer

Vesalius found out lots about the structure of the body and how it worked. He wrote down his findings so that other people could learn from him. He proved Galen wrong on several things and that is the main reason why he is so important.

Question 2: Answer

I don't think that Vesalius's contribution could have been made before the Renaissance for the main reason that dissection was banned for religious reasons before then. In the earlier periods, e.g. the Romans, people felt that if you cut up the body it would be disrespectful to the gods and the body might not go on to the next life. In the Middle Ages you would not go to heaven. Also in the Middle Ages people did not really want to dissect as they believed that God caused all diseases and so there was little point in finding out about disease. The only reason that some people might dissect would be to understand the work of Galen, but they did not look too closely. This leads on to another reason why Vesalius had to come from the Renaissance – until then no one would dare to criticise Galen as this would mean criticising a greatly respected Roman doctor or the Catholic Church that accepted his ideas as true.

Question 1: Examiner's Comments on Answer

This answer correctly identifies that Vesalius found out about the structure of the body, that he recorded his findings and that he proved Galen wrong, but there is virtually no detail to support the answer. Can you think of additional information that could be included? For example, what exactly did he find out about the body and how did he disprove Galen's work? By adding some more details you could easily increase your marks. I would give this answer 2 out of 5.

Question 2: Examiner's Comments on Answer

This answer explains dissection well and also talks about how the ideas of Galen were unlikely to be challenged before the Renaissance. The answer gives the Romans and Middle Ages as examples of periods when Vesalius's discoveries could not have been made. I like the way that the answer says that two points are linked (banning dissection in the Middle Ages and relying on Galen). I would give this answer about 6 marks out of 10.

How could you get higher marks? Well, the answer does not really talk about what was happening in the Renaissance. You could explain more about the idea of rebirth and the new thinking that led to renewed interest in medicine.

6 Practice Question

The answers above are on Vesalius. Now you give an answer on Harvey.

Edward Jenner – an 18th Century Turning Point

1

Topic Summary

Jenner is important in this study as he introduced the first real vaccination against disease. Not only did vaccinations save lives but the idea of injecting people with a disease to prevent them catching the full disease is the foundation of modern vaccinations. However, even Jenner did not fully understand vaccinations and he faced a lot of opposition.

2

What do I Need to Know?

- Edward Jenner was a country doctor and a member of the Royal Society. He was interested in the latest developments in science and medicine and knew that experimenting was vital to making progress.

- He heard about dairy maids in the country who had caught cowpox who then became immune to smallpox. He decided to test whether one disease prevented the other. Work like this had been done for years in other countries, but by using small doses of smallpox itself. This is called inoculation.

- Jenner injected a young boy called James Phipps with cowpox matter and then later injected him with smallpox matter. James survived and Jenner tested his ideas on a further 23 cases. All were successfully treated.

- Jenner named this process 'vaccination' after the Latin word *vacca*, meaning 'cow'.

- He was opposed by many doctors who were worried they would lose money because of his discovery. Other doctors, who were careless in their vaccinating and muddled up doses of smallpox and cowpox, sometimes killing the patient, were also against him. The general public were worried too. They did not understand the process and some of them were terrified of being injected with an animal disease.

- Jenner himself could not explain how vaccination worked, he just proved that it did.

- The government accepted his idea as they could see his success rate. They funded a vaccination clinic and later made vaccination compulsory.

Summary box

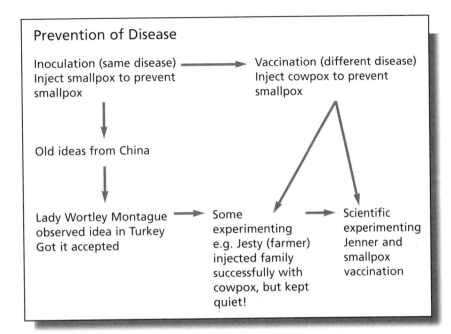

Prevention of Disease

Inoculation (same disease) ——————→ Vaccination (different disease)
Inject smallpox to prevent   Inject cowpox to prevent
smallpox   smallpox

Old ideas from China

Lady Wortley Montague ——→ Some   Scientific
observed idea in Turkey   experimenting   experimenting
Got it accepted   e.g. Jesty (farmer)   Jenner and
                           injected family   smallpox
                           successfully with   vaccination
                           cowpox, but kept
                           quiet!

This diagram should remind you that the idea of injecting people with a disease was already largely accepted as a result of the work of Lady Wortley Montague. This was inoculation. Jenner's work was really an extension of this. The difference was that he used a different disease and effectively prevented infection. This is vaccination.

3

What do I Know?

Explain why these are important in the development of medicine:

- Jenner's membership of the Royal Society
- The work of Lady Mary Wortley Montague
- Jenner's inability to explain how vaccination worked.

Once you have revised this topic thoroughly you should be able to answer most of these questions without using your notes. How many can you get right?

1 What helped Jenner to keep up to date with the latest developments in science and medicine?
2 From where did Jenner get the smallpox matter?
3 Who did Jenner inject with smallpox in his first experiment?
4 Why did he repeat his experiment 23 times?
5 What is the difference between inoculation and vaccination?
6 Who first brought the idea of inoculation to Britain?
7 Give two reasons that doctors had for opposing vaccinations.
8 Give two reasons that ordinary people had for opposing vaccinations.
9 If Jenner did not understand vaccination why did many people believe in his ideas?
10 How did Pasteur's discovery of the germ theory in the 1800s help the idea of vaccination?

My score........

4

Using the Sources

Look at this cartoon about the introduction of the smallpox vaccination and answer the questions below. Remember that cartoons are usually drawn to make a point. So the source might not be entirely reliable.

▲ **The cartoon shows people terrified of the use of cowpox as a vaccine against smallpox.**

> 1 What objections to smallpox vaccination can you see in this cartoon?
> 2 What other reasons did people have for opposing vaccination?
> 3 How reliable is this source as evidence for opposition to vaccination?

5

Exam Type Questions

In the exam some questions require you to write in detail about a figure in the history of medicine. Here is an example.

> 1 Describe how Jenner's discovery was made.　**(5 marks)**
>
> 2 Jenner did not understand why vaccinations worked. Why then was his work important in the history of medicine?　**(10 marks)**

**Question 1:
Answer**

Jenner discovered that smallpox could be prevented by injecting people with cowpox. He tested out his ideas first on a boy called James Phipps, who survived, and then 23 more times until he was sure that he was right. He called it vaccination after the Latin word for cow ('vacca'). He saved many lives as smallpox was often a fatal disease.

**Question 2:
Answer**

Jenner was important as he saved so many lives. Once people began to realise that vaccination worked more and more people were injected. The government in Britain and America realised how important this breakthrough was and gave him money. He was given £30,000 to open a vaccination clinic and smallpox vaccinations were made compulsory. In the 20th century smallpox has been wiped out completely as a disease. Jenner was also important as he gave ideas to others who could find out more about vaccinations.

**Question 1:
Examiner's
Comments on
Answer**

I would give this answer 2 out of 5. The information is correct about Jenner and it does contain a little exact detail. But look again at the question. The focus of the answer should be on how the discovery was made, i.e. what happened, how he did it, the process involved.

You would need to mention Jenner's knowledge about the immunity of dairy maids to smallpox and that people in the country knew that if you had contracted cowpox you did not catch smallpox. Jenner then tested out this idea by taking cowpox matter from Sarah Nelmes and injecting it into James Phipps' arm. Then he was given smallpox and survived. The answer did mention the tests that Jenner carried out. This was important – why? Check that you answer the exact question and don't just write down anything that you can remember. Have the last two sentences of the answer got anything to do with the question?

**Question 2:
Examiner's
Comments on
Answer**

This answer again contains some good detail about Jenner but you will notice that most of the answer refers to his immediate impact – the short term (saving lives). Although these ideas are true we are interested in the whole development of medicine and how Jenner may have contributed in the long term. The last sentence points to this issue but does not develop it. So I would only give this answer 4 or 5 out of 10. Jenner inspired Pasteur to investigate vaccinations with the new knowledge of the germ theory. Pasteur and Koch worked on other vaccinations once they had understood Jenner's work. Although Jenner's work did not lead directly to other developments for 100 years, it did fit in with the work of medical scientists in the 19th century.

Fighting Disease in the 19th and 20th Centuries

········1·········

Topic Summary

The 19th century brought industrialisation to Britain and with it over-crowded towns and cities and epidemics such as cholera and typhoid. Scientists worked hard to find out more about what causes disease. The real turning point was made by Pasteur, who discovered the germ theory of disease, and by Koch, who developed it. Twentieth century scientists, such as Domagk, Florey and Chain, developed drugs, such as penicillin. Now we have thousands of hi-tech drugs and skills to develop forms of genetic engineering, though not all the wonder drugs have been successful.

········2·········

What do I Need to Know?

Pasteur and Koch

- Before Louis Pasteur the most accepted theory of the cause of disease was that of spontaneous generation. This claimed that Germs caused disease and came from anything decaying.
- In 1861 Pasteur proved that germs in the air caused decay.
- Robert Koch, a German doctor, took Pasteur's work further and discovered that the germs also caused human disease. Pasteur and Koch were national heroes in their own countries, and were given research units to lead by their governments. This national rivalry helped spur them to further discoveries.
- Koch also identified the causes of different diseases by staining bacteria so that he could see them under his more powerful microscope. He discovered or 'isolated' the germs that caused tuberculosis (1882) and cholera (1883). This is a good example of science and technology joining up to make medical progress.
- Pasteur developed vaccines for diseases such as chicken cholera (1880), anthrax (1881) and rabies (1885). He could now understand Jenner's work on smallpox and apply the ideas to other diseases.

Other discoveries

- In 1928 Alexander Fleming discovered a mould called penicillium that killed several different bacteria. Fleming realised that this mould could kill germs but he did not have the skill in chemistry to purify the mould. But he did write a paper on his findings for others to read and study if they wished.

- Between 1939 and 1945 Florey and Chain developed Fleming's work by producing pure penicillin and getting it mass-produced. In order to do this they had to travel to America and won the cooperation of the wealthy drug companies. During the Second World War the British government realised that it needed the drug and provided funding to mass-produce penicillin, which was being used to treat soldiers by the end of the war. The most important aspect of penicillin is that it can kill many different germs.

- Behring found that anti-toxins in animals could help cure diseases and in 1909 Ehrlich discovered the first 'magic bullet' – a compound of arsenic that actually killed bacteria. He called it Salvarsan 606. This is an example of teamwork helping to make progress in medicine.

- Other drugs followed based on sulphonomides. In 1932 Gerhard Domagk discovered that a red dye called 'Prontosil' cured blood poisoning. Drug companies began to produce drugs based on the sulphonomide which was the part of Prontosil that killed the bacteria.

- Since the Second World War drugs have become big business with enormous profits. Vaccines have now been developed for polio, measles and whooping cough amongst others.

Problems with drugs

- Hi-tech drugs have not always been problem free. Thalidomide was a drug used for morning sickness during pregnancy, but it had not been thoroughly tested. This led to children being born with deformities (1959–62). Other problems with drugs today include addiction, cost, and the fear that the bacteria in the body might resist the effects of drugs. Scientists have not yet found a drug or vaccine for AIDS. Some older diseases, such a tuberculosis, are actually making a come-back.

Summary box 1

Cause and Cure of Disease – 19th and 20th Century Turning Points		
Causes in the 1800s	**Pasteur and Koch – the answer:**	**So what?**
• Dirt	(a) Germs in the air cause disease	Can now understand diseases
• Bad air/miasma	(b) Germs cause human disease	– and vaccinations
• Spontaneous generation		– and find more cures
		– and prevent diseases
		– and kill germs in operations

This diagram shows you the main changes in the explanation of disease between 1800 and 1900, and what a huge difference the germ theory actually made to medicine.

Summary box 2

In the 20th century more discoveries were made in the treatment of disease.

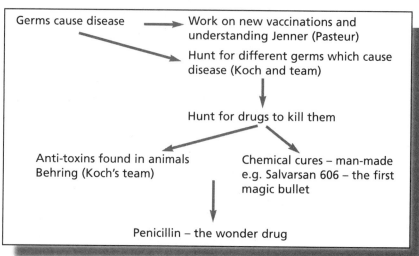

Germs cause disease → Work on new vaccinations and understanding Jenner (Pasteur)

Hunt for different germs which cause disease (Koch and team)

Hunt for drugs to kill them

Anti-toxins found in animals Behring (Koch's team)

Chemical cures – man-made e.g. Salvarsan 606 – the first magic bullet

Penicillin – the wonder drug

Add more details and dates to this summary to show how the killing of diseases has developed since Pasteur and Koch.

3

What do I Know?

Once you have revised this topic thoroughly you should be able to answer most of these questions without using your notes. How many can you get right?

Explain why these are important in the development of medicine:
- The germ theory
- Microscopes
- Salvarsan 606
- Penicillin
- Thalidomide.

How did Pasteur, Koch and other scientists lead the way to progress in:
- Public health
- Antiseptics and the work of James Simpson
- Changes in nursing and surgery?

1 What theory was widely believed to explain disease before Pasteur?
2 When did Pasteur discover the germ theory? Describe the experiments which proved his ideas.
3 Why was the germ theory so important?
4 What did Pasteur work on next?
5 What did Koch prove about the germ theory?
6 What did Koch work on next?
7 What was the first magic bullet?
8 What are anti-toxins and how are they useful in medicine?
9 How did Fleming discover the penicillium mould?
10 What exactly did Florey and Chain do that Fleming couldn't?

My score........

Surgery in the 19th and 20th Centuries

*....1.......................

Topic Summary

Operations before the mid-19th century involved great pain, sometimes masked by alcohol, and a likely chance of infection. The patient could also die of shock or blood loss. The advances in science and technology in the 19th century helped to stop most of these problems. Anaesthetics relieved pain, but had their own risks and problems. Surgeons became more confident, performed more and more complex operations, but there were no antiseptics at this time, so there were still risks of infection. The death rate actually increased until antiseptics were introduced.

Science in the 20th century brought more solutions. The discovery of blood groups meant that transfusions would now be successful. Surgeons can now use the advances in technology to do organ transplants, key-hole and laser surgery. But these operations are costly and hospitals face difficult decisions about how best to use their resources.

*....2.......................

What do I Need to Know?

- The chances of surviving surgery in the early 19th century were slim. James Simpson reckoned that soldiers on the battlefield of Waterloo had more chance of survival. Surgeons had to deal with problems of pain (no anaesthetics), infection (no antiseptics) and bleeding (few successful transfusions).

Anaesthetics

- The earliest anaesthetics used were laughing gas and ether. Dentists, such as Horace Wells, used nitrous oxide successfully for some time. Ether was very unpleasant for the patient and often people died for no apparent reason.
- In 1847 James Simpson discovered the benefits of chloroform while experimenting with chemicals at home with some doctor friends. He later used it for women giving birth, and the idea spread to other operations.
- Surgeons would now have far more time to operate, which meant they could do more complex operations. The death rate actually increased as mistakes were made, and the risk of infection was still great.
- Anaesthetics were strongly opposed by some doctors, nurses and the public. People were worried that it was against their religious beliefs to give a woman anaesthetics during childbirth. They believed that God had intended women to suffer the pain and that it was character building. Some doctors were worried about people dying because they were given the wrong doses and that allergic reactions were not understood.

Antiseptics

- In 1867 Joseph Lister began to use carbolic acid to kill infection in wounds. The use of the acid then spread to operating theatres in the form of sprays. These were quite unpopular with some doctors and nurses as they were messy and involved extra work. The benefits however became obvious when the death rates from infection began to drop rapidly.
- Once the germ theory had been accepted, antiseptics were then understood and surgeons also began to sterilise their equipment. Modern operating theatres are aseptic (germ free) areas. The equipment is sterilised and doctors and nurses wear masks and gowns.

Blood transfusions

- Blood groups were discovered in 1900. Until then blood transfusions were hit and miss affairs. Now transfusions were far more successful. This was especially important in war. During the Second World War emergency blood banks were set up for treating the wounded. This continued in peace time.

High-tech surgery

- In 1967 Dr Christian Barnard performed the first heart transplant. Multi-organ transplants are now commonplace.

This summary shows you the main developments in surgery that took place in the 19th century but also asks you to think about what difference each development actually made – how did it help?

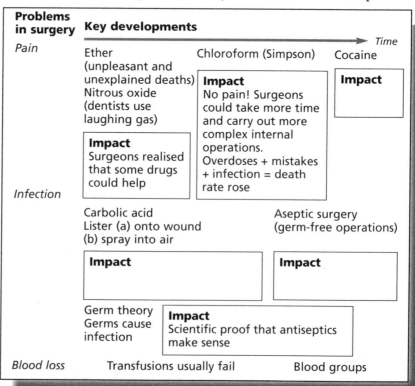

Tasks

Using the information in the summary box.
- Add dates to the key development.
- Make a list to show the impact of each development on surgery.
- Which of the developments relied on others to make a big difference?
- Make a list of the factors which led to each development.
- Make a separate list of facts/key words for each development.

3 What do I Know?

Once you have revised this topic thoroughly you should be able to answer most of these questions without using your notes. How many can you get right?

Explain why these are important in the development of surgery:

- Queen Victoria
- The sewage industry
- The germ theory
- The electron microscope
- The Crimean War
- First and Second World Wars.

1. What were the three main problems of early operations?
2. What was Robert Liston famous for?
3. What did Humphry Davy discover to help pain in 1799?
4. Name two problems with ether and chloroform.
5. Give two reasons why some people opposed the use of anaesthetics.
6. From where did Lister get his idea to use carbolic acid to kill infection?
7. Give two reasons why doctors and nurses opposed the use of antiseptics.
8. What is the difference between antiseptic and aseptic surgery?
9. Which war helped Florence Nightingale prove that women had an important role to play in nursing?
10. Name two operations performed today which rely on the very latest technology.

My score........

4 Exam Type Questions

These two questions require you to argue about the developments in surgery in the 19th century.

1. Anaesthetics revolutionised surgery. Were anaesthetics the most important development in surgery in the 19th century? **(10 marks)**
2. Why was so much progress made in surgery in the 19th century? **(10 marks)**

**Question 1:
Answer**

Anaesthetics were very important in the development of surgery. By using chloroform or ether the patients felt no pain and did not move during the operation, which distracted the surgeons. Patients would also be less likely to die from the pain and shock of the operation. Surgeons could take more time over operations and so carry out more complex procedures, such as internal operations. They could develop their skills and try out new techniques. However antiseptics are also crucial to successful surgery. Without antiseptics patients could easily become infected during the operation and gangrene could set in. In fact the death rate from operations actually went up before Lister discovered the use of carbolic acid in 1871. Surgeons carried out more operations and experimented but infection often killed the patient. Antiseptics and anaesthetics helped prevent this from happening.

**Question 2:
Answer**

The Industrial Revolution helped medicine with equipment and ideas. The sewage industry, for example, gave Lister the idea of using carbolic acid to kill germs. He used the acid directly onto wounds which healed much more quickly. He then sprayed it into the air during operations. Industry also made chemicals, such as chloroform, discovered by Simpson, as an anaesthetic. Science was also improving and education was becoming more important. So more doctors and surgeons were trained.

**Question 1:
Examiner's
Comments on
Answer**

This is a well argued and organised answer. I would give it about 7 out of 10 marks. It explains why anaesthetics were important but it also explains – in some detail – the role of antiseptics.

Can you think of more facts which could be added? How could you improve this answer? Was there any key development which was still needed? You could talk about blood transfusions and the problems with blood loss until blood groups were discovered.

**Question 2:
Examiner's
Comments on
Answer**

This answer mentions science, industry and education as reasons why surgery improved but only one of them is explained. Can you think of other facts or examples which could be used? What other factors were important? What about Pasteur and the germ theory? In most periods the key factors which caused change are all connected together so it would be good to show that you understand this. I would give this answer 5 out of 10.

_5_

**Practice
Question**

Having read the answers and the comments you should now attempt to answer the questions.

Public Health in the 19th and 20th Centuries

......1......

Topic Summary

Providing health services is part of the government's job even thought it requires a great deal of money and organisation. The Romans realised how important it was to have a healthy population but after their empire fell public health was virtually non-existent.

The Industrial Revolution brought a health crisis with increased disease and death, and forced the government to intervene.

By the end of the 19th century people accepted that clean water, sanitation and lighting were basic needs. By the mid-20th century people began to believe they should be cared for by the state in all aspects of their lives. In the 1990s some people are beginning to challenge this view.

......2......

What do I Need to Know?

Dirt and disease

- Industrialisation meant overcrowding. New houses were built with little attention paid to ventilation or sanitation. In conditions like these diseases spread easily.
- In the 19th century most people believed in *laissez faire*. They did not think that it was the government's job to interfere in their lives. Individuals should care for themselves.
- Many people did not realise the importance of being clean. The upper classes had no contact with the poor and did not realise how bad conditions were in the slums.

Epidemics and the call for action

- Cholera was a deadly epidemic which affected rich and poor. After epidemics in 1831–2 and 1848 the government introduced the first Public Health Act (1848). But once cholera died away so did the urgency to take any action.
- In 1854 Dr John Snow proved that cholera was carried in water. Pressure was put on water companies to clean their water supplies but they were reluctant to pay out.
- Pasteur's germ theory proved the importance of keeping clean, but the upper and middle classes were still reluctant to pay for the care of the working classes.
- In 1875 a second Public Health Act was passed making clean water, drains, sewers, and street lighting compulsory. *Laissez faire* was no longer so popular.

Government action

- In the 20th century governments became more involved. Wars, such as the Boer War, needed healthy people to fight and to work at home. The Liberal government (1906–16) introduced free school meals and health checks. Governments began to realise that combatting poverty led to less disease.
- The Liberals also introduced the National Insurance Act (1911) to give sick pay and medical care.
- After the Second World War the government provided more services, such as free hospitals, blood banks and ambulances. The welfare state was set up to look after all aspects of people's lives 'from the cradle to the grave'. This included financial help, such as family allowances.
- The National Health Service (NHS) was introduced in 1948. It was to provide a wide range of free medical services, from hospitals and doctors to dentists and vaccinations. It was funded by compulsory National Insurance. But some people were against it at first. A lot of doctors didn't want it. They wanted to be free from government control. And many people believed that this kind of help would make people lazy. Today there is much debate about whether the welfare state can actually be harmful to people by taking away their self-reliance.

Summary box

What sort of public health?

Limited 1830	Optional	Compulsory	Comprehensive (from the cradle to the grave)	
A few towns introduced drains, sewers, rubbish collectors and clean water	1848 Public Health Act, e.g. towns could set up Boards of Health if 10% voted. Short-term Central Board set up (for 5 years)	1875 Public Health Act, e.g. councils forced to provide basic sanitation and medical officers	Liberal reforms, e.g. pensions and National Insurance	Welfare state and NHS

Factors of change

Cholera kills rich and poor	All men get vote Government has to take action	Germ theory Proof about dirt and disease	Troops unfit for Boer War	WW1
Accurate recording of death figures Numbers shock government			Liberal government wants to stay in power	WW2

....3.............................

What do I Know?

Once you have revised this topic thoroughly you should be able to answer most of these questions without using your notes. How many can you get right?

Explain why these are important in the development of public health:

- The germ theory
- Industrialisation and urbanisation
- Cholera epidemics
- Edwin Chadwick
- John Snow
- The Boer War
- 1867 Reform Act
- Emergency ambulance and blood bank services in the First and Second World Wars.

1 Name a town/city that put the 1848 Public Health Act into action.
2 Give dates for two different cholera epidemics.
3 What was important about the 1848 Public Health Act?
4 How did John Snow realise that cholera spread through water?
5 Name one of two men who investigated the living conditions of the poor at the turn of the century and argued that poverty was connected to unemployment or low wages not laziness.
6 Which government introduced reforms such as pensions and free school meals between 1906 and 1914?
7 What does the phrase 'a country fit for heroes' refer to?
8 Name the health minister responsible for introducing the NHS.
9 What is the difference between the NHS and the welfare state?
10 What is the name of the organisation which fights disease on a world-wide scale?

My score........

....4.............................

Exam Type Questions

Here are two questions which might appear on your exam paper.

Look at Sources A, B and C.
1 Put these sources into chronological order. Use your knowledge and the sources to help you to explain your choice.
2 Why did it take so long for patients to get medical care free of charge?

Source A

The Public Health Act allowed authorities to pull down slums. There had to be a Public Health Committee in every district and they had to provide water, get rid of sewage, clear away rubbish and put a stop to unhealthy conditions in work places.

▲ **From a modern history text book.**

Source B

▲ A cartoon showing conditions in overcrowded towns.

Source C

Medical treatment should be made available to rich and poor alike in accordance with medical need and no other criteria. Worry about money in a time of sickness is a serious hindrance to recovery, apart from its unnecessary cruelty. The essence of a satisfactory health service is that the rich and poor are treated alike, that poverty is not a disability and wealth an advantage.

▲ Aneurin Bevan.

**Question 1:
Examiner's Hints**

Remember to mention all three sources and to explain why you have put them in the order you have. Explain this in several sentences, for each one use what is in the source and your own knowledge to back up your ideas.

**Question 2:
Examiner's Hints**

This is a 'factors' question which means that you should identify some and for higher marks know how they interconnect with each other. The question is basically asking what factors led to the introduction of the NHS and what factors held it back. Attitudes of people and governments will be an important part of this answer. What other factors influenced the introduction of free health care?

Themes, Factors and Turning Points

On the next three pages are summaries of the topics covered in your study. They divide your information into four areas (Cure and Disease, Anatomy and Physiology, Surgery and Public Health). We call these **themes**. In the exam you will be expected to answer questions on these themes. You will have to consider the pace and degree of change within each theme and which **factors** (war, religion, luck etc.) helped medicine to progress or hindered its progress. Some of these changes were so important that historians sometimes refer to them as a **turning point** in the history of medicine. Remember that medicine is a **development** study, so you have to know how much things develop and why!

Theme 1: Cause and Cure of Disease Through the Ages	
Prehistoric Times (Before 3000BC)	No written evidence. Ideas about the causes of disease were based on superstition and the supernatural.
Ancient Egypt (3000BC-400BC)	Still believed disease was caused by the gods. Some doctors, however, started using natural ideas and diagnosed symptoms.
Ancient Greece (800BC-400BC)	Had healing temples called Asklepions (supernatural). Hippocrates put forward a natural theory (the Four Humours). It was wrong, but it set medical development in the right direction.
The Romans (500BC-500AD)	Little regard for doctors. More interested in preventing disease than curing it. Illness was often treated with herbal medicines and opposites.
The Middle Ages (500AD-1500)	Parts of Western Europe were in chaos. Many medical books were destroyed. The ideas of Hippocrates and Galen were kept alive in the Middle East. Christian Church dominated people's lives. Many beliefs about the cause and treatment of disease were still based on the supernatural. Natural remedies based on the four humours also used.
The Renaissance (1500-1750)	Hardly any change. Treatments still based on a mixture of the supernatural and the four humours.
The Modern Period (1750-1900s)	Jenner discovered a vaccine for smallpox. Louis Pasteur proved the germ theory of disease. Koch identified specific germs which caused disease in humans. Pasteur also discovered other vaccines to prevent specific diseases. After 1900 chemical drugs which cured disease were discovered. Penicillin, the first antibiotic, discovered by Fleming and developed by Florey and Chain. A period of very rapid change. But recently some germs have become immune to antibiotics. Alternative treatments, such acupuncture and homeopathy, have become popular again.

Theme 2: Anatomy and Physiology Through the Ages

Prehistoric Times (Before 3000BC)	No written evidence so we have very little knowledge.
Ancient Egypt (3000BC-400BC)	Some knowledge of the inside of the body. Preserved the organs in special jars. Did not cut up the body to find out more, as this would have prevented it from going to the after-life.
Ancient Greece (800BC-400BC)	Dissected dead animals. Thought that the bone structure of the human body was like that of an animal.
The Romans (500BC-500AD)	Galen dissected apes and pigs. He thought that humans had the same anatomy, which was only partly true. Supported by the Church and his writings blindly followed for 1,500 years, even though he had made many mistakes. No one challenged his ideas until the Renaissance.
The Middle Ages (500AD-1500)	Galen's work was kept alive by Arab doctors. Islamic religion did not allow dead bodies to be dissected, so little new knowledge was found. In Western Europe in the late Middle Ages the Christian Church also would not allow human dissection. Galen's work was still followed.
The Renaissance (1500-1750)	Vesalius' *The Fabric of the Human Body* was a turning point. Vesalius dissected human bodies and proved Galen wrong. The power of the Church declined as old ideas proved wrong. In 1628 Harvey proved that blood was pumped around the body by the heart.
The Modern Period (1750-1900s)	X-rays were discovered by Roentgen in 1895. X-ray machines enable doctors to see the bones and the internal organs of the body.

Theme 3: Surgery Through the Ages

Prehistoric Times (Before 3000BC)	Archaeologists have discovered Prehistoric skulls which have been trephined to allow evil spirits to be released.
Ancient Egypt (3000BC-400BC)	Carried out simple operations, such as the cutting away of tumours. Descriptions recorded in papyrus medical books.
Ancient Greece (800BC-400BC)	Carried out minor operations. Surgical tools have been found.
The Romans (500BC-500AD)	Surgeons carried out operations on the battlefield. The remains of military hospitals and surgical tools have been found.
The Middle Ages (500AD-1500)	Military surgeons carried out simple operations on injured soldiers. Wine and hot cauterising irons used.
The Renaissance (1500-1750)	Paré forced to use a lotion of oil of roses, egg yolks and turpentine (a chance happening). Also used silk thread to tie up arteries, rather than stop the bleeding by using a cauterising iron.
The Modern Period (1750-1900s)	Three major problems – pain, infection and bleeding. Pain overcome by chloroform, infection by antiseptic and bleeding by the discovery of blood groups. The 20th century has seen the development of aseptic surgery and high-tech machinery. Period of rapid change in surgery. Factors which brought this about included the growth of industry, science, technology, communications, and the major wars.

Theme 4: Public Health Through the Ages	
Prehistoric Times (Before 3000BC)	There is no written evidence to inform us of ideas about public health in this period.
Ancient Egypt (3000BC-400BC)	No public health systems were provided by the government. But rich people were keen on personal hygiene.
Minoan Crete (2000BC-1380BC)	At Knossos in Crete there was an advanced system of drainage and water supply at the royal palace.
The Romans (500BC-500AD)	Romans needed healthy army to defend the empire. Government built public baths, latrines, sewers and aqueducts. First comprehensive public health system. The Romans wanted to prevent disease.
The Middle Ages (500AD-1500)	Roman system fell into disrepair. Time of regression. Medieval towns were filthy. Governments refused to clean them up. Monasteries, however, had washrooms and latrines. Many monks escaped the Black Death of 1347-9.
The Renaissance (1500-1750)	There was little improvement. Towns remained dirty. Rich people had better hygiene than the poor.
The Modern Period (1750-1900s)	The Industrial Revolution brought large towns, no sanitation and little fresh drinking water. No action because *laissez-faire*. Cholera epidemics frightened the government into temporary action. Chadwick highlights conditions of the towns. Discovery of the germ theory and extension of vote led to Acts of Parliament to make the towns cleaner. Liberal government introduced school meals and medical inspections, old-age pensions and National Insurance. Beveridge Report in 1942. National Health Service (NHS) set up in 1948.

Exam Type Questions: Cause and Cure of Disease

Now that you have studied your information and looked at it set out in themes, let's look at some questions and how they have been answered.

1 What changes in beliefs about the cause and cure of disease do Sources A and B show?
2 Why did this change take place?
3 Source C is 2,000 years after Source B, but it shows that beliefs about the cause and cure of disease seem to have stayed the same. How can this be explained?

Source A

> From about 600BC the Greeks began to worship Asklepios as the god of healing. At Epidaurus a massive temple was built called an Asklepion. The sick went there for Asklepios to cure them. Many other healing temples were built all over Greece.

▲ From a modern history book.

Source B

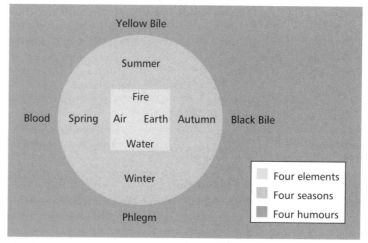

▲ A diagram showing the Theory of the Four Humours. This idea was suggested by Hippocrates, in about 400BC.

Source C

> 'More blood was let from the King and he was given medicine to make him vomit.'

▲ Sir Charles Scarburgh, the royal doctor, describing the treatment of Charles II in 1685. The King died from his illness after five days.

Question 1: Answer

Source A shows that the Greeks believed in the supernatural when it came to treating illness. Some people went to a healing temple called an Asklepion. They believed they would be cured by the gods. Source B is based on a natural idea. Hippocrates said that people fell ill if the four humours (liquids) were out of balance. For example, if you had too much phlegm you would have a cold. From this came the use of opposites. For a cold you would be given hot peppers as a treatment. So the change we can see between the sources is from superstitious beliefs to natural beliefs. People had begun to think through new ideas.

Question 2: Answer

The change from superstition to natural beliefs came about for many reasons. Hippocrates pioneered a completely new approach to medicine. The Greeks were civilised and well-organised people. They did not have to spend all their time thinking about survival. They had time to think. There were many philosophers who spent time observing and putting new ideas forward. Hippocrates thought about disease. He said that doctors should observe their patients – it was called clinical observation. If a patient's illness was observed, then a treatment could be prescribed.

Question 3: Answer

After the Greeks, the Romans did not come up with any new ideas about the cause and cure of disease. The Romans were more concerned about preventing disease than curing it. When the Roman Empire collapsed in about 500AD there was a period of regression. There were many wars and lots of medical books were destroyed. The Roman baths and aqueducts fell apart. Some of the Greek ideas were kept alive by the Arabs in the Middle East and then found their way back to Western Europe in the 13th century. By this time the Islamic and Christian religions were very powerful. Both said that Greek doctors, such as Galen, were right. No one questioned anything, so there was no progress. Charles II had the best doctors in England, but they still relied on treatments put forward by Galen and Hippocrates. No one came up with any new ideas about the cause and cure of disease until Louis Pasteur in the mid-19th century. He was able to discover that germs caused disease because technology had moved forward and there were good microscopes.

Question 1: Examiner's Comments on Answer

A good answer. The student has correctly identified the two different approaches to the cause and cure of disease and supported the answer with accurately recalled knowledge. Top marks could have been secured by mentioning that both ideas existed side by side during the Greek period.

Question 2: Examiner's Comments on Answer

This student has given two reasons for the change in beliefs and has a good understanding of the nature of Greek society at the time. This is shown by the reference to their being well organised and civilised. This, in turn, enabled people to think about the world. Mention of the fact that the Greeks had an empire and traded with other people and so had contact with a range of cultures and ideas would have deserved a very high mark.

Question 3: Examiner's Comments on Answer

A very good answer showing excellent understanding of the chronology of medicine. The student has identified several reasons which are placed expertly into historical context. In addition, the answer looks forward and shows that the key breakthrough in knowing about the cause of disease (the germ theory) is some way off. This answer shows how important it is to understand the chronology of the topic. I would give this full marks.

2

Exam Type Questions: Public Health

1 Why were there four cholera epidemics in the mid-19th century?
2 'The most important developments in medicine since 1850 have been in public health.' Say whether you agree with this viewpoint, making sure you support your answer with reasons.

Question 1: Answers

Student A

The Industrial Revolution meant the growth of towns. The towns were dirty - no clean water, overcrowded houses and filth in the streets. Cholera spread quickly in such conditions.

Student B

The Industrial Revolution caused the growth of filthy towns. The government did not do anything to clean up the towns. This meant that cholera spread quickly. The workers could not vote so they did not have anyone to speak up for them in Parliament. The houses were badly built. They were back to back and did not have toilets or clean water. Cholera took hold in these conditions.

Student C

During the 19th century the Industrial Revolution was taking place. Industrial towns, such as Liverpool and Manchester, sprang up. There was no such thing as planning permission. Builders wanted a quick profit so the houses were thrown up. The water supply and disposal of sewage was not good enough, so people lived in filthy conditions. Up to four hundred people would share one outside toilet. Linked to this was the fact that the government did not think it had any responsibility to clean up the towns (laissez-faire), so nothing was done. Even though Edwin Chadwick argued for cleaner towns he was shouted down by people who said it was none of his business. Ordinary people did not get the vote until 1867, so they could not put pressure on MPs to get something done. Not surprisingly cholera spread quickly in these conditions.

Question 1: Examiner's Comments

Student A

This is worth 3 to 4 out of 10. One reason is given and it is placed into context of the Industrial Revolution. The filthy conditions are linked to cholera.

Student B

This is probably worth 5 marks. The answer has given more than one reason and they are placed in the context of the Industrial Revolution. The reasons given tend to be isolated and are not linked together.

Student C

This answer is worth about 8 marks. The answer shows a good understanding of why cholera broke out and links the reasons into a chain of causation. Full marks could have been earned if it had been mentioned that it was not until the germ theory of disease that the importance of hygiene and clean water was fully understood.

Question 2: Answers

Student A

I agree because public health has made things cleaner. The Public Health Acts made town councils provide clean water and the National Health Service has brought in vaccinations against diseases like TB.

Student B

I do not agree with this. Public health has been important. Clean water supplies have helped to bring down the death rate and the welfare state has made sure that everyone has free medical care and things like old-age pensions, so people are looked after. But there are other things just as important. Anaesthetics, discovered by James Simpson, means that we have operations with no pain. The discovery of vaccines, such as smallpox by Edward Jenner, have also been important, as well as Lister's carbolic spray.

Student C

I don't think any one branch is more important as each branch of medicine supports the other to bring about a healthy population. Advances in public health has stopped the spread of disease and made people healthier. We now live much longer and if we do get ill there is the National Health Service and marvellous high-tech machines to make us better.

But the work of Pasteur in the period 1860-85 is just as important. Pasteur discovered the cause of disease and Koch went on to identify germs which caused disease in humans. Without the knowledge that there were germs in the air, Lister would not have come up with antiseptics and people would still have been dying from infection. Antiseptics then led to the development of aseptic surgery (germ-free operating theatres).

Once germs were identified then people realised it was important to keep clean to avoid illness. So more emphasis was put on making the environment cleaner. It also meant that scientists looked for ways of preventing disease and Pasteur came up with vaccines. Developments in each branch of medicine have worked together.

Question 2: Examiner's Comments

Student A
This answer is supported by accurate facts, but the question requires an answer which compares public health with other developments in medicine. This answer would score 3 or 4 out of 10.

Student B
This is a good comparative answer. It acknowledges the importance of public health, but also recognises that other branches of medicine have been vital. The answer is backed up with accurate recalled knowledge. This is probably worth 6 or 7 out of 10.

Student C
A very good answer, which illustrates that the branches of medicine (public health, surgery, cause and cure of disease) are interconnected. One change built on another to lead to medical development. The answer is very well supported, showing a good knowledge of the history of medicine. I would give this 9 out of 10.

Factors in Medicine

Here is a list of factors which have helped or hindered the progress of medicine through the ages. Some examples are given with each factor. You need to be able to write a little on each example to show its importance. You also ought to be able to add some more examples!

1	Factors helping development	
A	War	Romans needed fit soldiers. Good public health system. War wounds give surgeons like Paré opportunities. Crimean War helps nursing improve reputation and develop. Franco-Prussian War stimulates rivalry between Pasteur and Koch. First World War and blood transfusions. Second World War and plastic surgery and penicillin.
B	Chance	Paré runs out of oil. Chamberland injects chickens with chicken cholera germs. Pasteur and chance meeting with boy bitten by dog. Dr Hata re-tests Ehrlich's Compound 606. Fleming and penicillin.
C	Social and religious attitudes	Egyptian embalming helps knowledge of human body. Islamic belief in caring for sick and elderly. Work of Christian monks. Renaissance and rethinking of old ideas.
D	Communications	Invention of the printing press, Industrial Revolution and better transport. Electric telegraph and greater communication stimulates debate.
E	Governments	Romans have strong government organisation. French and German governments help Pasteur and Koch. Liberal government in Britain (1906–16). British and American governments fund work in penicillin. Labour government sets up NHS.
F	Science and technology	Scientific observation during Renaissance. Sciences develop during Industrial Revolution. Use of science in research, chemicals developed. Scientific and technological advances lead to machines and materials, e.g. microscopes, X-rays, plastic. Importance of electricity.
G	Individuals*	Hippocrates, Galen, Vesalius, Paré, Harvey, Jenner, Chadwick, Simpson, Nightingale, Seacole, Pasteur, Koch, Fleming, Chain, MacIndoe, Barnard. *It is very important to know about people who made a contribution in medicine. For each person write down the period he/she came from and a few facts about the contribution made.

2	Factors hindering development	
A War	The Vandals and Goths attack Rome. Loss of medical learning. Finance directed away from research and care.	
B Social and religious attitudes	Egyptians would not allow dissection. Religious attitudes hindered Galen. Religious groups prevented criticism of Galen and dissection. Belief in *laissez faire*.	
C Opposition to change	Conservative doctors oppose Galen. Opposition to Paré's methods and professional jealousy. Loss of income for doctors leads to opposition to Jenner's vaccine. Christians oppose use of chloroform. Conservatism resists any change. Opposition to nursing improvements. Objections to welfare state setting up 'nanny state'. Opposition to paying more taxes to help poor.	
D Lack of knowledge and technology	Lack of knowledge of anatomy and blood groups and the existence of germs. Before Industrial Revolution lack of technical knowledge prevented manufacture of effective microscope.	
E Governments	Until Middle Ages lack of organisation and stability prevented action. Belief in *laissez faire* meant opposition to action. Opposition to increased spending hindered progress.	

How Factors Work Together

On the next page is a diagram linking together the factors which helped Pasteur discover the vaccine for sheep anthrax. Study the diagram carefully and then answer these questions below:

Tasks

1 Was any one of these factors more important than the others? Write a detailed answer to this question, giving plenty of evidence and factual information in support.

2 Now build up some flow charts of your own which show factors working together to bring a development. Here are some ideas which you could work on:

Ambroise Paré and surgery (Individual brilliance, war, chance, communications, social attitudes)

Robert Koch and the hunt for microbes (Individual brilliance, communications, war, industry, science and technology)

Paul Ehrlich and Salvarsan 606 (Individual brilliance, chance, science and technology, the chemical industry)

The story of penicillin (Individual brilliance, chance, teamwork, war and government).

Pasteur and the Discovery of Vaccines

One factor on its own rarely produced change. Usually a change was caused by a number of factors working together. This diagram shows how several factors helped in Louis Pasteur's discovery of a vaccine for sheep anthrax in 1881.

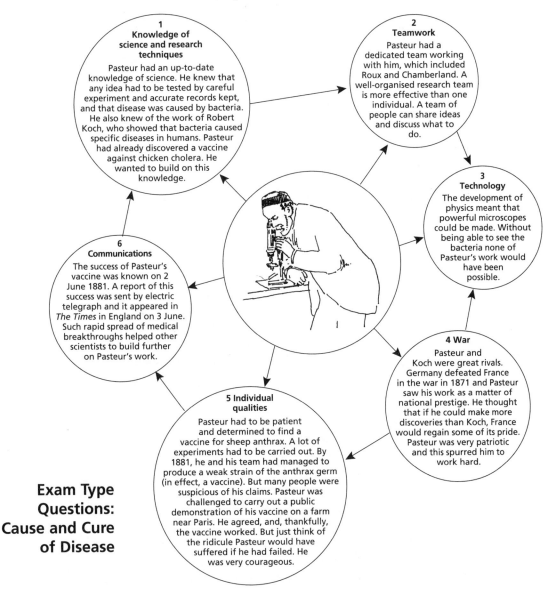

1 Knowledge of science and research techniques

Pasteur had an up-to-date knowledge of science. He knew that any idea had to be tested by careful experiment and accurate records kept, and that disease was caused by bacteria. He also knew of the work of Robert Koch, who showed that bacteria caused specific diseases in humans. Pasteur had already discovered a vaccine against chicken cholera. He wanted to build on this knowledge.

2 Teamwork

Pasteur had a dedicated team working with him, which included Roux and Chamberland. A well-organised research team is more effective than one individual. A team of people can share ideas and discuss what to do.

3 Technology

The development of physics meant that powerful microscopes could be made. Without being able to see the bacteria none of Pasteur's work would have been possible.

6 Communications

The success of Pasteur's vaccine was known on 2 June 1881. A report of this success was sent by electric telegraph and it appeared in *The Times* in England on 3 June. Such rapid spread of medical breakthroughs helped other scientists to build further on Pasteur's work.

4 War

Pasteur and Koch were great rivals. Germany defeated France in the war in 1871 and Pasteur saw his work as a matter of national prestige. He thought that if he could make more discoveries than Koch, France would regain some of its pride. Pasteur was very patriotic and this spurred him to work hard.

5 Individual qualities

Pasteur had to be patient and determined to find a vaccine for sheep anthrax. A lot of experiments had to be carried out. By 1881, he and his team had managed to produce a weak strain of the anthrax germ (in effect, a vaccine). But many people were suspicious of his claims. Pasteur was challenged to carry out a public demonstration of his vaccine on a farm near Paris. He agreed, and, thankfully, the vaccine worked. But just think of the ridicule Pasteur would have suffered if he had failed. He was very courageous.

Exam Type Questions: Cause and Cure of Disease

Exam Type Questions: Change

1 'Many of Galen's ideas about the human body were wrong, so he is not important in the history.' Do you agree with this view? Give reasons for your answer. **(10 marks)**

2 This question tests whether you understand about the pace of change in medicine.

'The pace of change has varied throughout the history of medicine.' Do you agree or disagree? Explain your answer. **(10 marks)**

Question 1: Answer

Galen was very important. He was a famous Greek doctor who lived between 130 and 201AD. He was interested in anatomy. He wrote many books about it and his ideas lasted for over a thousand years. Galen was not allowed to dissect human corpses. People thought this was wrong. Galen was not put off. He dissected apes and pigs instead. This gave him some good ideas. The mistake he made was to think that animals and humans were the same. But, at least he found something out.

Question 2: Answers

Student A

I agree. Sometimes things change quickly but then you get times when there is hardly any change.

Student B

This is right. Medicine was making progress until the fall of the Roman Empire. Then there was a turn for the worse. Things really slowed down. In fact, they went backwards. The Romans had helped public health by building aqueducts and latrines, but when the empire collapsed these things fell down. By the Middle Ages, conditions in towns were worse than they had been in Roman times.

Student C

I strongly agree. You only have to look back through time to see this viewpoint. The Egyptians and Greeks both moved medicine on a bit. The Egyptians had some knowledge of the human body because of embalming and the Greeks came up with the Theory of the Four Humours. So these periods showed a moderate pace of change. Then there was further progress when the Romans developed their public health system. This then fell into decay during the Middle Ages. The Roman Empire fell and there were centuries of stagnation. Nothing happened. The Renaissance speeded up the rate of change with the work of Vesalius, Pare and Harvey. But even these breakthroughs were not fully put to work until further things had happened. For example, the circulation of the blood did not bring immediate change, as people did not know about blood groups. In the last 150 years the pace of change has been very quick. The Industrial Revolution helped to bring rapid change in the cause and cure of disease (the germ theory) and also antiseptics and the welfare state. Perhaps the rate of change at the moment is slowing down. They still haven't found a cure for AIDS and some germs are now resistant to some of the drugs doctors use.

Question 1: Examiner's Comments

This answer sees Galen as important despite the fact that he made some mistakes. It says he is important because his ideas lasted for a long time and because he at least found some things out. It is probably worth 5 or 6 out of 10. To score higher the answer needs to say how Galen was important because he laid the foundations and allowed others to build on and challenge his ideas – and give examples.

Question 2: Examiner's Comments

Student A

The answer shows some understanding of development. But there is no supporting evidence from the history of medicine. Only worth 1 or 2 out of 10.

Student B

This answer shows some understanding of the development. It mentions a period of regression and slow change and has some accurate supporting knowledge. Probably worth about 5 out of 10.

Student C

A comprehensive answer, which shows an excellent understanding of the pace of change varying in medicine and fully supported with knowledge. Worth nine 9 of 10.

Now answer this question.

> Why has there been such rapid change in medicine in the last 150 years?

Hints for success

Give as much supporting knowledge as possible and to show how factors such as the Industrial Revolution, war, teamwork, chance and individuals have worked together to bring about the germ theory, antiseptics, anaesthetics, vaccines, drugs and the welfare state.

2

Exam Type Questions: The Role of the Individual

Here are more practice questions. See how they are assessed, then answer them yourself.

---

1 What contribution did Joseph Lister make to the development of medicine? **(6 marks)**

2 Was Lister's contribution to medicine welcomed at the time? **(7 marks)**

3 Was Lister's skill and talent all that was needed for him to be able to make his contribution to medicine? Explain your answer. **(12 marks)**

Question 1: Answer

Joseph Lister made a very important contribution to the development of medicine. He was the person who introduced antiseptics into the operating theatre in the 1860s. Lister read about Pasteur's discovery of the germ theory. He realised that germs must be causing people's wounds to get infected after operations. Perhaps there was something which would kill the germs. Lister also knew that carbolic spray was used to disperse the smell from the sewers in Carlisle. He decided to use it during and after his operations. He used it on an eleven-year-old boy who had broken his leg. It worked. The boy's leg healed without getting infected.

The carbolic acid was sprayed into the air and on to bandages. Deaths from infection in the operating theatres soon went down dramatically. About twenty years later, surgeons went a stage further by using aseptic surgery. This meant keeping the operating theatre sterile. Surgeons and nurses started to wear masks, gowns and rubber gloves.

Question 2: Answer

You would think that such an important breakthrough would have been readily accepted. But Lister faced great opposition to his carbolic spray. The acid irritated the skin and eyes of the surgeons and nurses. Some nurses thought the spray was too much bother to use and did not like the smell of it. Some people were not convinced by the germ theory. They could not see any germs in the air and wondered if Pasteur was right. Other people just did not want to change; they were too used to the old methods.

Question 3: Answer

Lister was a very skilful man. He was the Professor of Surgery at Glasgow University. He was interested in medicine and was always trying new things out. He was a determined man. Even when doctors opposed his carbolic spray he did not give up and kept on using it. So I think this was the main reason why he was able to make his discovery.

Question 1: Examiner's Comments on Answer

This is a very good answer, showing clear knowledge of Lister's work. It is worth 6 out of 6. The reason for this is that the student has seen the importance of the word 'development' in the question. Lister's contribution to medicine led to other developments – antiseptic to aseptic surgery. The answer has plenty of supporting detail which makes it worth full marks. An answer which just talked about carbolic acid spray would have scored 3 to 4 marks only, depending on the quality of the supporting knowledge.

Question 2: Examiner's Comments on Answer

A solid answer showing a quite good understanding that many changes in medicine were held up by opposition. The supporting material is accurate and, therefore, I would give this 5 out of 7.

To get more marks the answer needed to mention that, in time, the opposition was overcome. Deaths from infection went down and people began to realise that the spray worked. To get over the problem of skin irritation, rubber gloves were introduced.

Question 3: Examiner's Comments on Answer

This question is a classic opportunity to show an understanding that several factors of change worked together to bring medical development. This answer misses out because it agrees with the question and only talks about Lister's personal qualities. It is worth about 4 marks out of the 12 available.

To score more marks answers need to show an understanding that there were other factors involved, such as Pasteur's germ theory, communications, technology (microscopes), and the chemical industry (carbolic spray). These should be discussed and compared with Lister's individual talent. The very best answers will attempt to show how the factors are interconnected and fit together.

Practice Questions

Now it is your turn! Answer these questions.

1 Explain an example of war helping the development of medicine.
2 Explain an example of war hindering the development of medicine.
3 Explain an example of chance helping the development of medicine.
4 Has war always brought progress to medicine? Explain your answer.
5 'Religion has helped the development of medicine more than it has held it back.' Do you agree with this viewpoint?

Hints for success

- Your answers for questions 1, 2, 3 should include as much supporting material as possible. Remember that the questions ask you to explain, not just describe. For example, you must say how war played a part. The best answers will also take into account the word 'development' and explain what came from the examples you have chosen.
- Remember to look at both sides of the issue when answering questions 4 and 5. Consider times when these factors have helped and times when they have hindered development. Then draw a conclusion.

Turning Points

Some developments were so important that they are looked upon as turning points. A turning point is usually one event which turns ideas, beliefs and knowledge in a different direction. After a turning point things are never quite the same again. Here is one example of a possible turning point.

The Fabric of the Human Body 1543: How Vesalius turned the study of anatomy in the right direction.

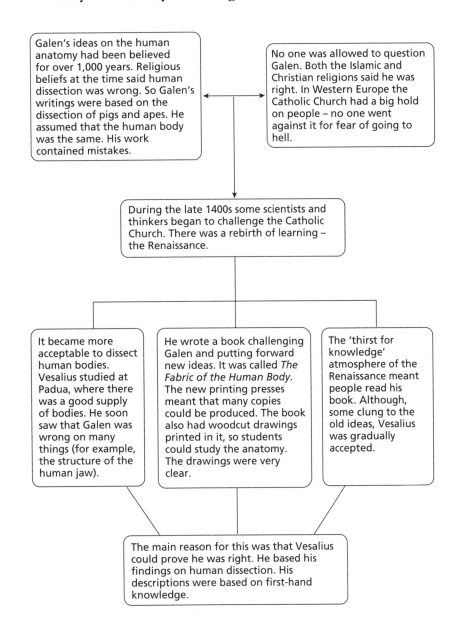

Galen's ideas on the human anatomy had been believed for over 1,000 years. Religious beliefs at the time said human dissection was wrong. So Galen's writings were based on the dissection of pigs and apes. He assumed that the human body was the same. His work contained mistakes.

No one was allowed to question Galen. Both the Islamic and Christian religions said he was right. In Western Europe the Catholic Church had a big hold on people – no one went against it for fear of going to hell.

During the late 1400s some scientists and thinkers began to challenge the Catholic Church. There was a rebirth of learning – the Renaissance.

It became more acceptable to dissect human bodies. Vesalius studied at Padua, where there was a good supply of bodies. He soon saw that Galen was wrong on many things (for example, the structure of the human jaw).

He wrote a book challenging Galen and putting forward new ideas. It was called _The Fabric of the Human Body_. The new printing presses meant that many copies could be produced. The book also had woodcut drawings printed in it, so students could study the anatomy. The drawings were very clear.

The 'thirst for knowledge' atmosphere of the Renaissance meant people read his book. Although, some clung to the old ideas, Vesalius was gradually accepted.

The main reason for this was that Vesalius could prove he was right. He based his findings on human dissection. His descriptions were based on first-hand knowledge.

Construct Your Own Flow Chart

Another important idea which could be looked upon as a turning point was the germ theory of disease. Make a large copy of the diagram below. Research and fill in the boxes with relevant information.

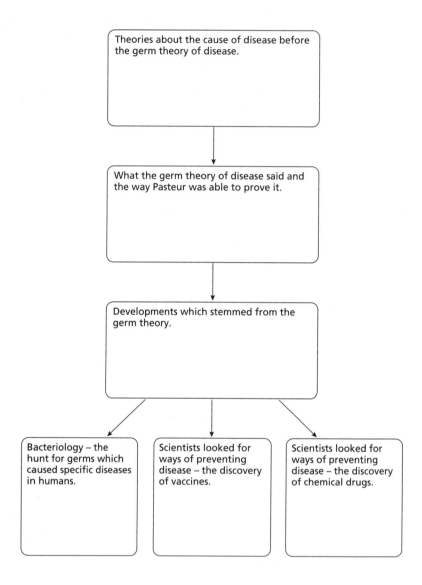

Theories about the cause of disease before the germ theory of disease.

What the germ theory of disease said and the way Pasteur was able to prove it.

Developments which stemmed from the germ theory.

Bacteriology – the hunt for germs which caused specific diseases in humans.

Scientists looked for ways of preventing disease – the discovery of vaccines.

Scientists looked for ways of preventing disease – the discovery of chemical drugs.

Use your flow chart to write a long answer to this question:

> Why might the germ theory of disease be considered a turning point in the history of medicine?

Hints for success

Define a turning point. Say what was believed before the germ theory was put forward. Say what the germ theory was about. Explain the developments the germ theory led to.

Source-based Exercise in Medicine

Three of the examination boards, OCR, SEG and Edexcel set source-based investigations on Medicine. Here as an example of the type of exercise you might be asked to tackle in the examination.

How far did standards of nursing improve in the second half of the 19th Century?

Read the sources and answer the questions. Then look at the student answers given and the examiners' comments that follow. At that point you should be able to return to your own answers and improve them.

---

1 Study Source A. What can we learn about nursing in the nineteenth century from this source?

2 Study Sources A and B. How similar are these two sources? Explain your answer.

3 Study Source C. Does this source prove that standards of nursing in Britain had improved by 1862? Explain your answer.

4 Study Sources D and E. Which of these two sources do you think would be most useful to a historian studying the history of nursing in the nineteenth century? Explain your answer.

5 Study all the sources. 'By the end of the nineteenth century standards in nursing had improved dramatically.' How far do Sources A-E support this view?

Background information

During the second half of the nineteenth century a number of important changes were made in the way that nurses were trained. Much of the credit for these changes has been given to Florence Nightingale, though other people, such as Mary Seacole, played an important part too. Just how much difference did these changes make to the standard of nursing in Britain?

Source A

'I do not agree that the nursing establishments of our hospitals are inefficient, or that they are likely to be improved by any special institution for training. Nurses are in much the same position as housemaids and require little training or teaching beyond that of poultice-making (such skill is easily acquired), the enforcement of cleanliness and the attention to patients' needs. This proposed hospital nurse training scheme has not met with the support of the medical profession.'

▲ J.F. South, President of the Royal College of Surgeons, commenting in 1851 on a proposal to set up a training school for nurses.

Source B

They are sexually, constitutionally and mentally unfitted for the hard and unending work, and for the heavy responsibilities of general medical and surgical practice. Women might become midwives, but in an inferior position of responsibility as a rule. I know of no great discovery changing the boundaries of scientific knowledge that owes its existence to a woman. What right have women to claim mental equality to men?

▲ An extract from an article about the role of women in medicine. It was written by a male doctor in the medical journal, *The Lancet*, in 1870.

Source C

You are expected to become skilful:
1 In the dressing of blisters, sores, wounds and applying poultices and minor dressings.
2 In the application of leeches, externally and internally.
3 In the management of helpless patients, i.e. moving, changing, cleanliness, preventing and dressing bed sores.
4 You are required to attend at operations.
5 To be competent to cook gruel, arrowfoot, egg flip puddings, drinks for the sick.

▲ Part of the instructions to newly trained nurses at Florence Nightingale's School for Nurses at St Thomas's Hospital in 1862.

Source D

▲ A cartoon, drawn in 1879, showing a nurse at the bedside of a patient.

Source E

'Some of the nurses were the best type of women, clever, dutiful, cheerful and kind – and endowed above all with that motherliness of nature which is the most precious attribute of a nurse.'

▲ A matron, working in a hospital in Edinburgh, describes her nurses.

Source F

A public fund raised £44,000 and the money was used to start up the Nightingale School of Nursing at St Thomas's Hospital in London. It was here that standards were laid down for the training of nurses. Trainees had to be disciplined and willing to work hard. They served a one-year probationary period and then trained for a further two years in order to qualify. Other training schools followed Nightingale's example and by 1900 the number of nurses in Britain had risen from 24,000 in 1861 to 61,000.

▲ An extract adapted from *Medicine Through Time* by Bob Rees and Paul Shuter.

Question 1:
Answer

We can learn a great deal about nursing from this source. First of all we can learn that nursing was considered not much of a job because somebody as important as the President of the Royal College of Surgeons says that nurses are nothing more than housemaids who do a little bit of poultice-making. We also learn that there is an attempt to improve nursing standards by providing a training scheme (this must be the one that Queen Victoria asked Florence Nightingale to set up) and that there was opposition to it from conservative doctors and surgeons.

Question 2:
Answer

The sources are not similar at all. One is saying that nursing is a low standard job and the other is saying that women are no use in the medical profession because they are not equal to men. They are talking about different things.

Question 3:
Answer

This source could be looked at in two ways. On the one hand, we could say that improvements have been made because nurses are to attend at operations and apply leeches, which shows they were important. And they were being told to make sure that they looked after patients properly, by dressing their bed sores etc. The fact that these things were laid down as rules shows that they can't have been done properly in the past.

On the other hand, these were just instructions and we don't know that everyone followed them. After all, this is just one training school and who is to say the nurses all did it? And what about all those nurses who were 'newly trained'. They were probably as bad as ever.

Question 4:
Answer

It's difficult to answer this because they are both useful. Source D is useful for telling us that bad practices still survived in nursing in 1879 (though the cartoon talks of 'old style', so the new style must have been better). Source E is useful for telling us that there were good nurses in Scotland around the same time (though the fact that the matron says 'some of the nurses' suggests that others weren't good). Mind you we would have to be careful because the sources could be biased. One is a cartoon and the other is by the matron of the hospital.

Question 5: Answer

I think that some of the sources do show that by the end of the nineteenth century standards had improved, but others don't.

Obviously the best source for proving this is Source F. It is from a book on medicine and so is probably well-researched and reliable. It shows that trainees had to work hard and there was an increasing number of training schools. Source E suggests standards improved as well, though we have to be careful about whether these things actually happened and how widespread improvements were likely to be.

Source A is not about improvements and Source B is really about women as doctors (though it shows that anti-women feelings hadn't changed by 1870). Source C shows that there were some very poor nurses around in 1879, but it is a cartoon and may well have been drawn in that year to show what nurses used to be like. Anyway I would need to know who drew the cartoon and why before I could say what this source really shows.

Question 1: Examiner's Comments on Answer

This is a very good answer. It does not concentrate on the superficial importance of the source (it tells us that nurses looked after patients, made poultices etc.) but instead focuses on what we can learn about attitudes and the status of nursing from this source. The comment on South's position is a very good example of how to use information in captions. Note that the question does not say 'How much can we learn?', so there is no need to talk about the source's limitations.

Question 2: Examiner's Comments on Answer

What the candidate says here is true, but the answer would not score high marks. When you are asked 'How similar?' it is because the examiner thinks there are similarities and differences. In this case the differences are the most obvious (one is talking about nurses and the other is saying why women can't ever be doctors). But there are similarities. They are both saying that women do not make much of a contribution to medicine and are both putting forward the conservative anti-women argument that had to be overcome before women could play their full part in medicine. Our candidate needs to say that, as well as noting the differences, to score high marks.

Question 3: Examiner's Comments on Answer

A very good answer. The candidate notes the improvements that are likely to have been made but also realises the difference between instructions and reality. I particularly like the way the candidate realises that one good training school doesn't mean improvement in nursing everywhere.

Question 4: Examiner's Comments on Answer

This is only a partial answer. It makes some good points on what the sources are useful for, but does not consider what they don't tell us. The candidate realises that if sources are not reliable this affects their usefulness, but there is no attempt to show why being a cartoon or an account from the matron would be a problem. Answers must always be developed to explain what is being said. This one isn't.

Question 5: Examiner's Comments on Answer

This is a good answer. The candidate comments on all the sources and realises that what is required is more than just looking at the detail in them. We also need to consider their reliability. A source which is completely unreliable can't be used to support a hypothesis.

The American West, 1840–95

Depth Study: Summary

This depth study focuses on what changes took place on the Great Plains. The years studied represent a turning point for the native American Indians, the Plains, and America as a whole. Tribes of native American Indians had lived on the Plains for hundreds of years, but between 1840 and 1895 their traditional way of life came to an end. The seemingly 'Wild West' became home to thousands of new settlers, who adapted and tamed the land to survive.

The changes on the Plains were not just brought about by the different groups of people. Other factors had an impact, such as the railroads, technological inventions and the government policy of 'Manifest Destiny'. When the railroads were built the Plains were changed forever. People travelling from east to west saw for themselves the potential of the land. The government also encouraged the settlement of the Plains. Even Europeans were encouraged to emigrate from their homelands and settle there. The government wanted America to be fully settled and secure as a country.

This settlement brought the American Indians and the whites into conflict. You will need to consider why the whites and the Indians clashed so much and how the settling of the Plains caused problems of law and order as other groups clashed with each other.

By the end of our period (1895) the Plains were certainly no longer the Great American Desert. They had been successfully 'tamed' and were full of people fulfilling the 'American Dream'. This study helps you to revise these changes in more detail and how and why they occurred.

Life on the Plains – the Plains Indians

There were actually many different nations of Native American Indian in different regions of North and South America. Our case study looks at those nations living on the Plains and in particular the Sioux. Their lifestyle was drastically changed as a result of events over a 50-year period.

Most Indian customs stemmed from their belief that land and animals should be treated with respect as they were equal to humans. They were nomadic in order to hunt. Survival was more important than laws, so polygamy was practised.

The lifestyle and beliefs of the Indians were opposite to those of the whites who saw the Indians as uncivilised and barbaric. White Americans believed that there was one God who wanted them to farm the land, and not to 'waste' it as the Indians did. Clashes between the two groups were inevitable, especially once the whites decided that they wanted the Plains for themselves.

.........2..........

What do I Need to Know?

You will need to understand the Indian way of life and their beliefs and how their religion influenced everything they did. You will need to know how the whites and the Indians did not understand each other and why they were so different.

- The Indians believed that land, animals and humans were all equal. This meant that they could not farm the land or animals and had to survive by hunting. To do this they had to follow the buffalo, so they could not settle, and lived in tepees.
- With the need to move on the old or sick would leave or be left to die, often quite willingly. This was called exposure.
- The Indians often took on more that one wife (polygamy) in order that all the women might be provided for and have children. Christians found this uncivilised and unacceptable.
- The Indians believed in the 'Great Spirit', called Waken Tanka by the Sioux. They communicated with the spirits through medicine men, visions and dances. When you died your spirit would go to the 'Happy Hunting Ground'.
- The Indians could not afford to lose members of the band in battles. Warfare therefore involved surprise attacks and raids which the whites thought were cowardly. A 'brave' could demonstrate his courage by touching the enemy, called 'counting coup'. This was considered much more brave than fighting one to one and risking death.

- Enemies were sometimes scalped to prevent their spirit from going to the Happy Hunting Ground. The whites saw this as particularly barbaric.

Summary box 1

Try to explain how all these aspects of Indian life are connected and add some more links if you can.

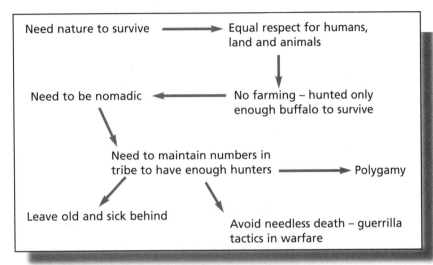

3

What do I Know?

Once you have revised this topic thoroughly you should be able to answer most of these questions without using your notes. How many can you get right?

Explain why the following are important in the history of the Plains Indians:

- Polygamy
- The tepee
- Scalping and counting coup
- Exposure.

(Some ideas might be important because of what the whites thought about them, as well as how they helped the Indians to survive on the Plains.)

1　What was the Sioux name for the Great Spirit?
2　Where did Indians believe that they went to when they died?
3　Give two different ways of contacting the Great Spirit.
4　Put these groups in order from biggest to smallest: tribe, band, and nation.
5　On what did the Indians rely for food, clothing and shelter?
6　Which was considered to be more important by the Indians – land or animals?
7　Why didn't Indians kill all the animals in a hunt?
8　Why did whites think that land should be farmed?
9　What did Indian warriors do to enemies to prevent their souls from moving to the next life?
10　What was the name given when elderly members of the tribe were left/moved away to die?

My score ....

4

Using the Source

Examine the engraving and then answer the questions that follow.

▲ **An Indian scalping a soldier, engraved in 1892.**

> 1 What impression of the Indians do you get from this picture?
> 2 Use your knowledge to explain why a white man and an Indian would disagree over this interpretation.

Hints for your answers

1 Identify the impression the source gives you of the Indian. Think of adjectives that sum him up: brutal? brave? cowardly?

2 Back up each idea that you have with proof from the source.

3 Explain why an Indian and a white man would probably choose different words to describe the scalping. Use your knowledge. What did Indians believe about scalping?

Early Settlers on the Plains

Topic Summary

In 1840 the Plains were known as the Great American Desert and no white Americans imagined that anyone could live there successfully. The Plains were dry, barren and wild. The first white Americans to have contact with the Plains either worked on the edges of them or travelled through them on the way to settle on the West Coast. Land on the West Coast was far more fertile or gold could make you rich. The mountain men trapped animals in the Rocky Mountains to the west of the Plains. The pioneers and miners made the dangerous journey across the desert in search of a better life for themselves. Although the three groups did not settle on the Plains they had contact with the area on their journeys and began the process of opening up this vast land to others.

What do I Need to Know?

As none of these groups settled directly on the Plains they are not major case studies for us. What you do need to know, however, is what they were doing crossing the Plains, how they coped and what messages they gave to other people about their experiences. The mountain men had a lot of insider knowledge that they could spread. If the pioneers and miners were successful in the West then many others would eventually follow.

Mountain men

- The job of mountain men was to trap and hunt animals, such as beavers, for their fur. To do this they had to know the mountains and surrounding areas very well.
- Sometimes the mountain men worked alongside Indians and some even married Indian women. Comparisons can be made with the Indians in the way that they dressed, their reliance on animals for survival and their knowledge of the land. Cartoons from the time even joked about these similarities.
- Once a year trappers, traders, fur companies (such as the Rocky Mountain Fur Company), and sometimes Indians met together for a 'trade fair' called a 'rendezvous' (the French for 'meeting'). Representatives from the companies would hear stories about the land west of the Plains and this news would be spread by the traders as they travelled up and down the Missouri River.

Pioneers

- The first group of pioneers travelled to Oregon in 1839, seeking a new life for themselves on the other side of the Great Plains. Land was becoming more scarce in the East as the population grew. Also there was a financial crisis in 1837 which caused bankruptcies and unemployment.
- The journey across the Plains in simple wagons was full of dangers such as lack of water, blizzards, running out of food, huge rivers and sometimes attacks by hostile Indians. As the pioneers were unfamiliar with the land they often employed mountain men to guide them across it. Some groups did not survive the journey. One example was the Donner party, of which half died in blizzards.

Miners

- In 1848 gold was discovered in California. A rush of people followed trying to make their fortune. Some were experienced miners, others just men looking for a lucky break or an adventure.
- When the surface gold ran out in California miners moved to the gold mines of the Rocky Mountains. There were strikes in Idaho in 1860, Arizona in 1863 and the Black Hills of Dakota in 1874. The Black Hills were special Indian hunting grounds but the gold rush brought in a flood of miners and devastated the Indians (see page 108).
- Professional miners worked for companies and settled in temporary towns on the Plains. They relied on the railroad to bring in supplies and take out gold. This demand increased the investments in the railroads.

Summary box

This is a summary of where the early settlers on the Plains moved from and how they encouraged further movement.

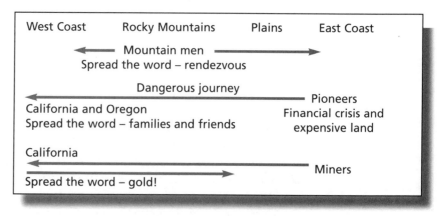

You will notice that the miners actually break the normal pattern of moving to stay in the West – they moved eastwards when the gold ran out and so had direct contact with the Plains.

Task Copy and complete this chart to show details for each of the three groups of early settlers on the Plains.

Group	Why they had contact with the Plains	How/where they lived	What difference they made to the Plains
Mountain men			
Pioneers			
Miners			

3

What do I Know?

Once you have revised this topic thoroughly you should be able to answer most of these questions without using your notes. How many can you get right?

1 Name one fur trading company that many mountain men worked for.
2 Give two similarities between mountain men and Indians.
3 Give two examples of contact between mountain men and other white Americans.
4 Name one place on the West Coast that the pioneers were heading for.
5 Give two reasons why the pioneers travelled to the West Coast.
6 Name two problems that the pioneers faced on the journey across the Plains.
7 In one famous party only half the group actually made it across the Plains. What was the name of the group leader?
8 When was gold discovered in California?
9 Which gold strike in 1874 meant that miners rushed into Indian hunting grounds?
10 Which major technological breakthrough was speeded up by the demands of the miners for resources?

My score......

Explain why these are important in the history of the Plains:

- The basic lack of water and the extreme temperatures on the Plains
- The Rendezvous
- Letters from pioneers to families in the East
- Gold runs out on the West Coast.

4

Using the Sources

Source A

▲ A cartoon with one mountain man saying to another: 'I took ye for an injun'.

Source B

▲ This cartoon shows some of the financial problems faced by people in the East.

---

1 Why would mountain men be 'mistaken for an injun' as this cartoon jokes? Use your knowledge as well as the picture in your answer.

2 What contact was there between the mountain men and the Indians?

5

**Exam Type
Questions**

Here is one question that might appear on your paper. You will need to use Sources A and B on page 84.

Use Sources A and B and your knowledge to explain why pioneers took the dangerous journey across the Plains to the West. **(10 marks)**

Student A

Pioneers went across the Plains because mountain men told them to and life was bad in the East. They wanted a new start.

Student B

Pioneers risked their lives to cross the Plains as they were so desperate for a new life. They could not afford land in the East where the population was great and there was also growing unemployment. In the West there was so much more land, it was cheaper and families heard stories from friends about how fertile it was. There was money to be made.

**Examiner's
Comments on
Answers**

Student A

This student has tried to use the sources and is generally correct about life in the East, but is confused about mountain men and has included no real detail. I would give this 2 marks out of 10.

Student B

This student does explain a little about conditions in the East but does not really use Source B to help. The answer does not talk about the attraction of the West Coast – what pulled the pioneers there – but in order to get higher marks more details could have been added. I would give this 5 marks out of 10.

The Mormons

........1........

Topic Summary

The Mormons were a different type of settler. They came from states to the east of the Plains but then chose to live in the West, in the unfertile Salt Lake Valley. They travelled across the Plains like the pioneers, but perhaps they had less choice. Non-Mormons were suspicious and feared the Mormons. They were opposed to the Mormon belief in polygamy and resented Mormon successes. The second Mormon leader, Brigham Young, knew that unless they moved far enough away from other white Americans they would face opposition wherever they settled. After the Mormons had been forced out of three states (Ohio, Missouri and Illinois), where they had tried to settle, Young decided they should cross the Plains to find their own place to live. When they reached Salt Lake Valley they worked hard to make their 'Zion' ready for Christ's Second Coming. Salt Lake became a prosperous, largely self-sufficient city and eventually, on giving up polygamy, an independent state of America.

........2........

What do I Need to Know?

In order to understand why non-Mormons were so suspicious of Mormons you will need to remember their beliefs and where they came from. Joseph Smith's role as founder of the religion is vital to their history. You will need to trace their movement across the states of Ohio, Missouri and Illinois and why they failed to settle in each area. On Joseph Smith's death Brigham Young emerged as leader. He confirmed this by making the harsh, but wise, decision to move to such a remote place as Salt Lake Valley, and successfully organising the journey across the Plains. You will need to know his actions before, during and after the journey. You will also need to consider how important he was in the development of the Mormon religion. Other factors helped to make Salt Lake City a success and you should be able to explain these and compare their importance.

The beginning and Joseph Smith

- The story is that in 1823 Joseph Smith was shown some plates buried by an angel called Moroni on a mountainside. The plates were translated to him by the angel. They told the story of battles between different tribes of Israel. The angel and his father Mormon were the only survivors and they predicted that the finder of the plates would prepare God's kingdom on earth for Christ's Second Coming.
- The Mormons therefore believed that they were chosen to build 'Zion' – God's 'heavenly city'. Joseph Smith gained more and more supporters and they settled in Kirtland, Ohio. But they were driven out of Kirtland when successful Mormon banks lost money in a crisis in 1837 and non-Mormon investors blamed the Mormons for the problems.

- The Mormons moved to Independence in Missouri and soon became successful again. Mormons worked very hard, and they gave 10 per cent of their money to the Mormon Church which could buy more and more land. Again non-Mormons resented their success and felt threatened by their increasing numbers. They were also highly suspicious of the Danites, who were the Mormon secret police organisation. Many Mormons were arrested and the others had to leave Missouri for Illinois.
- In Illinois they had more success building their own town, which they called 'Nauvoo'. Here they actually became an independent political state and made their own laws. But the non-Mormons of Illinois felt threatened by the Mormons' increasing power and were disgusted by the practice of polygamy.
- Joseph Smith had led the Mormons to success, but his polygamy and political ambitions led to war in Illinois. He declared that he would stand as a candidate in the Presidential elections and the non-Mormons decided that enough was enough. Smith was killed by a mob in 1844.

Brigham Young and the move to Salt Lake Valley

- It was now up to Brigham Young to lead the Mormons out of Nauvoo. He decided to risk moving across the Plains to Salt Lake Valley, which was unfertile and desolate. No one would ever want to challenge them there.
- Young organised the trip across the Plains in military style, training teams and breaking up the journey into sections. The advance party reached the Great Salt Lake in 1847.

The organisation of Mormon society

- The success of the journey confirmed Young as leader. On arrival he divided the land into equal sections for people to work. It belonged to everyone and was run by the Church which prevented arguments. He set up a committee to plan the sharing out of water and the digging of irrigation ditches to enable the land to become fertile enough to farm.
- Young realised that to become self-sufficient they needed more skilled workers, so he set up a Perpetual Emigration Fund to bring in Mormons from elsewhere.
- The Mormons wanted to be totally independent, but the government would only let them become a territory, not a 'free' state. Young was even replaced as governor in 1857. In the same year there was a massacre of 150 migrants. People blamed either the Danites or the Indians, but the government decided that either way they wanted a peaceful solution. Mormons were finally allowed to live under their own laws, but did not become a totally independent state until 1890, when they compromised and gave up polygamy.

Summary box

This summary shows where the Mormons attempted to settle on the Plains and why they were forced to move at each stage.

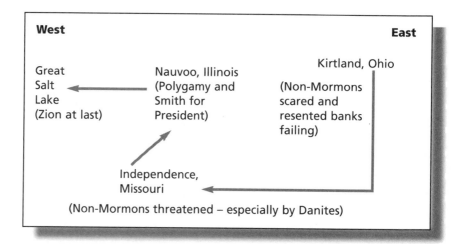

Were the Mormons chased out for the same real reasons at each town? Remember that the Mormons started out on the Plains but then moved across them to Salt Lake Valley – so they did not settle on the Plains.

3

What do I Know?

Once you have revised this topic thoroughly you should be able to answer most of these questions without using your notes. How many can you get right?

Explain why these are important in the history of the Mormons and the Plains:

- Mormon belief in polygamy
- Mormon success in banking in Kirtland
- Joseph Smith running for President
- Brigham Young
- Mormon belief that they were God's chosen people.

1 Who wrote the Book of Mormon?
2 Name the first area that the Mormons settled in.
3 Name the Mormon secret army/defence group.
4 Name the second place they settled in.
5 Name the last place they settled in before making the journey across the Plains.
6 How did Joseph Smith die?
7 Who chose to take the Mormons to Salt Lake Valley?
8 In what year did they make the journey?
9 What was the name of the fund set up by the Mormons to bring in skilled Mormons to Salt Lake City?
10 What did the Mormons have to give up in order to become an independent state?

My score.....

Using the Source

Look at the source and answer the questions that follow.

▲ An American cartoon making fun of polygamy.

1 Use this picture and your knowledge to explain what most non-Mormons thought about the Mormons.
2 Do you think that this cartoon gives a true picture of the Mormons?

Hints for your answers

- Start with the message in the source. Explain the point it is making.
- What other reasons did non-Mormons have for opposing polygamy?
- Explain each reason using your knowledge.
- Remember that cartoons are often exaggerated but have to be based on some element of truth in order for them to be understood.

Cattlemen and Cowboys

The history of the cattle industry is in different stages. It began with the driving of cattle from Texas through the Plains to the markets in the North. Then cattlemen and cattle buyers started meeting at cattle towns or cattle markets which grew up when the railroads were built across the Plains. This encouraged more people to settle on the Plains. New technology, such as the wind pump, and the successes of migrant settlers encouraged the cattle industry to the Plains and ranches were set up. At first the ranches were open, with cattle roaming free to find water holes and food.

The cattle industry reached its peak in 1880. But there were now too many cattle, causing their price to fall and ruining many ranches. The fate of open ranching was sealed by bad winters in 1885-6. Ranching changed after this. It became more like 20th century farming, with enclosures surrounded by barbed wire.

Cattlemen and homesteaders did not live easily side by side. Clashes between them showed that conflict on the Plains was not just between whites and Indians.

2

What do I Need to Know?

You need to know the different stages of the cattle industry and why it changed. You will also need to know what the successes and problems of the industry were, and the roles of individual entrepreneurs like Goodnight, Loving and McCoy. Western movies made the cowboy into a figure of myth: he was a hero, a troublemaker, an adventurer. You will need to know what they really did and what sort of people became cowboys and why. Their job also changed as the cattle industry became more settled.

The beginning and the long drives

- The cattle industry began in Texas with the Spanish settlers. The first long drives of cattle began in 1837. During the Civil War (1861-5) cattle had been allowed to roam free and their numbers grew rapidly. There was a lot of money to be made selling beef to the industrial cities of the North.
- The long drives North were dangerous and exciting. The cowboys risked attacks by hostile Indians and cattle rustlers. They had to face bad weather and lack of water, and opposition from local homesteaders who did not want their own cattle to be infected by the Texas Fever carried by the Longhorn cattle. Charles Goodnight and Oliver Loving showed that long drives were profitable and that they could sell beef to the army camps and Indian reservations.

Growth of ranching and cattle towns

- Several factors led to the end of drives and the beginning of ranching on the Plains. Indians started charging cattlemen for the right to cross the land given to them by the government. New homesteads began to block the cattle trails. Cattlemen decided that it would be easier to drive their herds to railheads so that they could be taken further north and east in rail wagons. Joseph McCoy built a market town called Abilene to buy and sell cattle on the Plains. Other cattle towns grew up along the path of the railroads. We will look at problems in these towns on page 103.
- At first ranches were 'open', in that the land was free and unfenced. Ranchers competed with one another and with settlers over land and water holes. Cattle rustling was also a cause of conflict between cattlemen and homesteaders. We will look at this conflict later on page 104.

Boom, bust and change

- The cattle industry boomed as population increased, but the number of cattle grew to be far greater than the demand for them. And there was more competition for grass and water. The hot summer of 1886, which killed the grass and dried up the watering holes, was followed by the harsh winter of 1886-7, when snow covered whatever grass there was. The cattle boom finally came to an end.
- The remaining ranches began to use new technology. They used wind pumps to supply water and barbed wire to fence off their areas. The days of the long drives were over. Ranch hands now had to mend fences and care for cattle on closed ranges.

Summary box This summary should help you remember how and where the cattle industry changed.

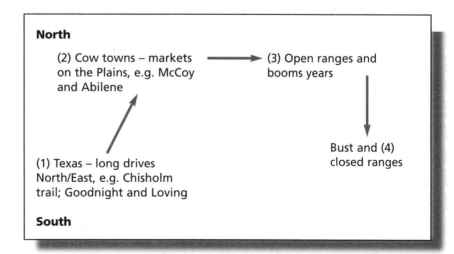

3

What do I Know?

Once you have revised this topic thoroughly you should be able to answer most of these questions without using your notes. How many can you get right?

Explain why these are important in the history of the cattle industry and the Plains:

- The Civil War
- The railroad
- Expansion in the North
- The Indian reservations
- The bad winter of 1886–7
- Barbed wire.

1 Where did the first drives take cattle to and from?
2 What happened to cattle during the Civil War?
3 Name the two famous cattlemen who made a success of the long drives.
4 Who founded Abilene?
5 What factors helped to make ranching on the Plains possible?
6 Who did Illif sell meat to?
7 When were the boom years for the cattle industry?
8 When did the cattle industry collapse?
9 Name two factors that contributed to the closure of many ranches.
10 Name two issues that caused conflict between cattlemen and homesteaders.

My score……..

4

Using the Sources

Source A

▲ **Longhorns stampeding.**

Source B

▲ **Cowboys on the closed range.**

> 1 Does Source A give a realistic impression of the work of the cowboy?
> 2 Compare Source A with Source B. Which situation shown in the sources came first in the cattle industry? Use your knowledge and the sources in your answer.

5

Exam Type Questions

Here are two of the sorts of questions you might be asked in an exam. Read the answers carefully and then see what the examiner thought of them.

> 1 Briefly describe how the work of a cowboy changed between 1840 and 1890. **(7 marks)**
> 2 The Great Plains were dry and barren, not the ideal environment to breed cattle. Why then did the cattlemen settle there? **(9 marks)**

Question 1: Answer

At first the job of the cowboy was full of adventure and excitement. They had to look after the cattle on the long drives, from Mexico to the North and East of America. They had to watch out for stampedes, bad weather and rustlers, and guide the herds along the trails. They might even be attacked by Indians. At the end of the period the job of the cowboy had changed. They didn't even need as many skills. Their job was more like a farmer as they mended fences on the ranches and fed and rounded up cattle. They did not get to travel any further than the nearest market or rail head.

**Question 2:
Answer**

> The cattlemen settled on the Plains because they had problems with the long drives and it made more sense to farm the cattle nearer to the markets. The situation on the Plains had improved with wind pumps and barbed wire so it was easier for them to be successful. The railway also made life easier for the cattlemen and they knew that there was a lot of money to be made in the business.

**Question 1:
Examiner's
Comments on
Answer**

This answer is well organised in that it writes about the early period and then how the job had changed. Details of the problems with long drives are included and some specific information about life being a range hand. I would give this answer at least 4 out of 7 marks. To get full marks I would look for an answer based around the question of what actually changed and not one just describing both periods separately.

**Question 2:
Examiner's
Comments on
Answer**

This answer is also well organised. Notice how it talks about the problems with the long drives, then why the Plains weren't that bad really, and about the potential profits to be made. The focus of the argument is fine – factors which caused the industry to change. However, there are two main weaknesses with this answer. First, there is not much detail or specific evidence to support the ideas. Information about the problems with Indian attacks, opposition from settlers fearful of Texas Fever, stampedes etc. could be included in the first section. Details about the railroads and other technology would also be helpful, for example, when barbed wire was introduced and which was the first railroad. The second weakness is that although the answer given is correct it is not explained. The ideas are a little vague and they are also listed more than developed. How exactly did wind pumps and barbed wire mean that ranches on the Plains could be successful? The secret to a good depth study answer is to explain your ideas well and support them with specific details. I would give this answer 4 out of 9 marks.

6

**Practice
Questions**

Here are extra exam questions for you to complete.

> 1 Why did the cattle trade eventually go bust?
> 2 How important were individuals, like Goodnight and McCoy, in creating a boom in the cattle industry?

The Railroads, Technology and 'Manifest Destiny'

....1......................
Topic Summary

The homesteaders and cattlemen had their own reasons for wanting to settle on the Plains. You will look at these motives separately. They were, however, encouraged and helped by other, external factors, which were influential in changing the Plains forever.

....2......................
What do I Need to Know?

The railroad companies

The first railroad company was built in 1869 by the Union Pacific Railroad Company and the Central Pacific Railroad Company. By 1893 there were six companies connecting East and West. The government gave the companies free land, which they then used or sold off to settlers and investors, further encouraging business. The companies wanted settlers to use the trains instead of wagons and once people moved onto the Plains, many more rail services would be required. So the railroad companies advertised the potential of the Plains and even sold cheap tickets. Pamphlets and posters were sent to the East and West, and to Europe to encourage foreign settlers. The advertising often exaggerated the potential for farming on the Plains.

The government's policy of Manifest Destiny

The term 'Manifest Destiny' refers to the American belief that it was their God-given right to control and rule the whole of North America. America had gained this land by treaties and wars with France, Britain and Mexico, and the government was worried that unless the vast lands were settled any of those countries might try to regain territory. In order to be safe and successful the lands had to be filled with loyal, hard-working, white Americans. This was only right and proper and would fulfil the 'American Dream'.

The government actively encouraged settlement by giving away cheap or free land to settlers. They did the same for the railroad companies who would take people, supplies and new ideas from East to West Coast and advertise the potential of the Plains. Putting this policy into action did have one major barrier: the Indians.

Technology and inventions

Many new settlers to the Plains soon found that the stories about life there were not always accurate. Many returned to the East or West. But those who stayed would eventually reap the enormous benefits of simple improvements in technology.

1 Barbed wire, patented by Joseph Glidden in 1874, made crops safer from stampeding cattle. Homesteaders and cattlemen now had to work hard to share watering holes (before wind pumps came into use). As you know this did not always happen peacefully.

2 Wind pumps made drilling for water easier and crops had a chance of surviving.

3 Mechanical reapers, threshers and other farm machinery enabled homesteaders to survive. They were expensive at first, but by the 1880s were cheap enough to be easily replaceable. They were brought to the new towns by the railroads.

Summary box

A summary of how the Plains came to be settled with the help of the railroads and the government.

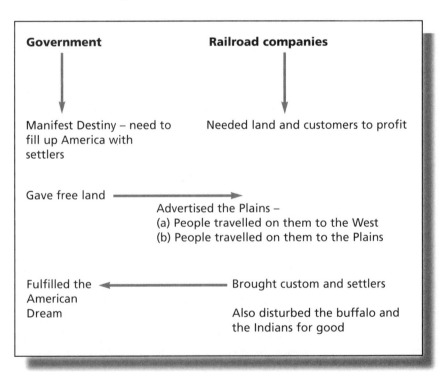

This diagram shows you how the railroads were important in helping the government to fulfil the Manifest Destiny policy, and how they were helped by the government itself – it was a mutual relationship.

96

3

Using the Source

▲ An advertisement by a railroad company offering to sell land to settlers.

What does this source tell us about the situation on the Plains in 1875?

Hints for your answer

Use your knowledge of the railroad companies and the settlers (and the government) to answer the question. These smaller questions might help.

- What did the railroad company do to encourage settlers to buy land?
- Why did the company want to sell all its land?
- Why did people want to settle there?

The Homesteaders

1

Topic Summary

The homesteaders fulfilled the American Dream. Together with the cattlemen they achieved the unachievable by settling on the Plains and making the land fertile enough to support them. Their story is one of risk-taking and hardship, although they were given incentives by both government and railroad companies. They knew little about the realities on the Plains, but like the pioneers and the Mormons they wanted a better life, and were desperate enough to take huge risks.

The homesteaders took advantage of new technology to help them to manage the land. Many did not make it, but the success of others opened the flood-gates to mass migration, which led to the race for land and the end of the Indians' way of life.

With the Plains filling up with white Americans, the Indians could not live their nomadic lifestyle. The homesteaders backed the army's efforts to move the Indians onto reservations as a way of getting rid of troublesome neighbours. This support for Manifest Destiny meant that the American Dream would be fulfilled.

2

What do I Need to Know?

You need to know why the homesteaders chose to move onto the Plains. They were also attracted to the Plains without knowing what conditions were really like. The homesteaders' story is one of success, but huge problems had to be overcome. Learn the details of their problems and their solutions and be able to compare their situation with that of other groups.

Why did they move to the 'Great American Desert'?

- Life in the East was increasingly hard for many Americans. Land was becoming more expensive and jobs harder to come by. This was also happening on the West Coast, where the pioneers had settled and claimed most of the land. Many wanted the opportunity to start a new life and farm their own land. Europeans, including Irish Catholics, were also arriving on the Plains to settle, having fled from religious persecution or economic problems in their homelands.
- The railroad companies encouraged settlers to move to the Plains. As you have read on page 95 they advertised across America and Europe. In this way they also were a factor in pulling the migrants West.

Goverment help

- The government was another strong factor encouraging the settlement of the Plains. Remember that this suited the Manifest Destiny to fill the land with white Americans. They made land available in the Homestead Act of 1862, allowing settlers to claim 160 acres of land and pay $30 after five years, making the land their own. This would ensure that the Plains settlement was a permanent one.

How the homesteaders survived on the Plains

- When the homesteaders realised 160 acres would not support the average family, the government passed the Timber and Culture Act in 1873. This doubled the amount of land homesteaders could claim, but there was a catch. They had to plant trees on half of it.
- Surviving on the Plains was incredibly difficult. The homesteaders had to cope with whatever resources were available. This meant building sod houses from earth rather than wood. They could not dig drainage ditches to get water as there were no streams or rivers to tap. In Nebraska, for example, there was a drought between January 1859 and November 1860.
- The homesteaders found solutions to most of their problems. Russian emigrants knew about 'Turkey Red', a strain of wheat which could grow in the harsh conditions. The use of dry farming saved rainfall from being immediately evaporated by the sun. Railroads brought machinery and supplies, and general stores were set up in the new towns. Homesteaders could also sell any surplus crops they did manage to grow. The Timber and Culture Act meant that in the long term wood would be available on the Plains.
- Wind pumps and mechanical reapers were examples of new technology that revolutionised the work of the homesteader. Land could now be made fertile enough to produce enough to survive. Barbed wire made land safe from stray cattle, although this caused huge problems as we will see on page 104.

The essential role of women

- Women were vital to survival on the Plains. They used any resources available to care for their families. As there was no wood for fuel they had to collect dried cow and buffalo dung to burn. These 'cow chips' burnt quickly so they had to collect large amounts. They had to feed their families with limited food supplies and also had to cope with the bugs and dirt that lived in the sod house.
- Some young women became school teachers and often lived with a family in the area. It was important that the children of the West were taught to be civilised American citizens.

- In 1889 the Oklahoma land race (see p 108) finally allowed settlers to occupy the remaining Indian territory, and so the American Dream was almost complete.

Summary box

This is a summary of the problems faced by the settlers on the Plains and how these were overcome. Some of the solutions have been left for you to fill in.

Aspect	Problems for the homesteaders	Solutions
Water	• Lack of rain and water • Droughts • Wells expensive and not very effective • Could not irrigate • Crops would not grow	• Wind pumps • • Dry farming
Size of land	• 160 acres not enough to support a family • Too much land to farm/handle on your own • No spare labour/men to help	• Timber and Culture Act • •
Machinery	• Would break easily • Spare parts difficult to get and expensive	• Railroads made spare parts easier to get •
Crops	• Maize and spring wheat would not grow well • Not enough to support family and make a profit	• Turkey Red – a hardy crop from Russia •
Fencing	• Cattle trampling on precious crops • Arguments over boundaries with neighbours	• •
Others	• Fires destroy crops • Grasshoppers/Rocky Mountain locusts • Indian attacks	•

Tasks

- Make a list of your own solutions and fill in the gaps.
- Add details to each point and explain how they were a problem or how the solution worked.

3 What do I Know?

Once you have revised this topic thoroughly you should be able to answer most of these questions without using your notes. How many can you get right?

Explain why these were important in the history of the homesteaders and the Plains:

- Religious persecution and economic problems in Europe
- The railroads
- Women
- The Timber and Culture Act
- Barbed wire
- Wind pumps.

1 Name one group who moved onto the Plains to escape religious persecution.
2 Why didn't the homesteaders move to the fertile land on the West Coast like the pioneers had done?
3 Name two things that attracted them onto the Plains.
4 What did they have to build houses from?
5 What was the nickname for the settlers who built these houses?
6 What was the main problem for farmers on the Plains?
7 What was the name of the crop which actually grew well in such extreme conditions?
8 Name and date the Act that the government passed to give the settlers more land to use?
9 What did the homesteaders use to fence off their land?
10 What did the homesteaders have to use for fuel?

My score............

4 Using the Source

Study the source and then answer the questions that follow.

▲ This painting shows settlers on their way to the Plains.

1 What impression does this painting give about the journey to the Plains?
2 Would the government have approved of this painting? Use your knowledge to explain your answer.

5

Exam Type Questions

Here is the sort of question you might be asked in an exam. Read the answers carefully and then see what the examiner thought of them.

> The homesteaders and the Indians were the largest groups to live on the Plains. Although the Plains were dry and hostile both groups managed to survive. Did they use the same methods? **(8 marks)**

Answer

The homesteaders used technology to help them, such as the wind pump and farming machines. They used what they could get from around them and had to make do. They got new ideas about growing different crops and rushed outside to turn over the soil each time it rained. This helped to keep in the moisture rather than let it be dried out by the sun. The Indians followed the buffalo which gave them everything they wanted. They travelled around the Plains and left their old people or sick people behind them. They believed that the land was equal to them and so they had to respect it.

Examiner's Comments

This answer describes both groups and does talk about methods used to survive. What would be better is if many more details were included and if an actual comparison was carried out. Remember that comparing groups is not best done by describing them one at a time. Like earlier answers this one does not explain points even though the student seems to understand. Can you spot which points could be developed more? They do actually explain one method used by the homesteaders – can you work out which one it is? A better answer would say whether the methods used were similar or different and then go on to explain and give examples. I would give this answer 4 out of 8 marks.

6

Practice Questions

Here are extra exam questions for you to do.

> 1 How important was the government in encouraging the homesteaders to settle on the Plains?
> 2 How successful were the homesteaders in taming the Plains?

Law and Order on the Plains

....1.......................

Topic Summary

Settling a new area brings many problems. We are used to governments and councils organising our health care, education and our law and order. For the settlers on the Plains there was no such support. Many towns were for miners or the cattle industry and therefore had few permanent inhabitants. In the early years of the cow towns, such as Dodge City, the cattlemen and cowboys wanted entertainment after the hard work of the long drives. Some turned to crime, or at least fighting with rival gangs. Whilst the towns on the Plains were relatively small, the inhabitants were reluctant to pay local taxes to set up efficient systems of law and order, and some gangsters took advantage of this situation.

....2.......................

What do I Need to Know?

The stories of shoot-outs, bank robberies and cattle rustling are well known from the movies. You need to know the real extent of the problems and the real reasons for these problems. Look at what the settlers did themselves to try and improve law and order. How successful were they? The best known example of a violent conflict between homesteaders and cattlemen is the Johnson County War, so you will need to know the causes and consequences of this clash.

Myth and reality of the 'Wild West'

- The famous examples of problems of law and order in the 'Wild West' are the shoot-outs, bank robbers and corrupt sheriffs, gamblers and prostitutes of the Western movies. All of these existed to a certain extent, but remember that the Western romanticised these stories. For example, the money stolen in bank robberies was relatively small in amount.

Problems of law and order

- The real problems took time to be solved as settlers arrived before the government could set up a system of law and order or plan towns carefully.

- The areas being policed were a long way from each other, and had too much land to control. Sheriffs were often untrained and unskilled for the job.
- Claim-jumping and disturbances over land claims in the 'public domain' were common, but after the Homestead Act in 1862 claims had to be registered, so less speculation and corruption could take place.
- Miners courts were set up to put people on trial and deal with any problems. Often these failed. People simply refused to accept their verdict.

Vigilantes

- Settlers resorted to forming vigilance committees and took the law into their own hands. The vigilante groups acted quickly and dealt with problems such as cattle rustling. In Bannack, Montana, vigilantes got rid of 100 highway robbers in 1865. Often they made mistakes, hanging or lynching innocent people.
- An example of a vigilante group getting out of control was in Johnson County where Ella Watson and her partner Jim Averill were hanged for cattle rustling, without a trial. They were innocent. She was a prostitute who was sometimes paid in cattle. The hanging sparked off the Johnson County War in 1862.

The struggle between cattlemen and homesteaders

- The Johnson County War was the worst clash between homesteaders and cattlemen. It was about cattle rustling, but it was also a power struggle for control of the county.
- Cattlemen and homesteaders often argued over the use of watering holes and cattle rustling. Some cattlemen went against the law and cut barbed wire fences to get to water.
- These were hard years for the cattle industry and the cattlemen hired gangs of gunfighters to hunt out any rustlers. The homesteaders decided to protect themselves. The show-down had to be broken up by the army, ordered in by President Harrison. The battle between the two sides showed how ineffective the law and order system was.
- As more and more settlers moved on to the Plains a system of law and order evolved.

Summary box

This chart shows at a glance the main problems and solutions offered by the settlers to the problem of law and order on the Plains.

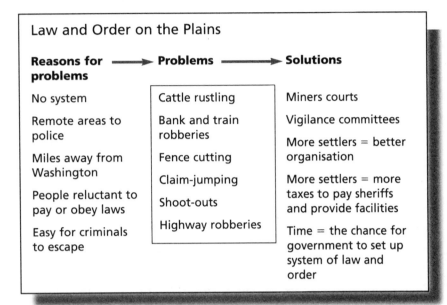

Law and Order on the Plains

Reasons for ⟶ Problems ⟶ Solutions
problems

Reasons for problems	Problems	Solutions
No system	Cattle rustling	Miners courts
Remote areas to police	Bank and train robberies	Vigilance committees
Miles away from Washington	Fence cutting	More settlers = better organisation
People reluctant to pay or obey laws	Claim-jumping	More settlers = more taxes to pay sheriffs and provide facilities
Easy for criminals to escape	Shoot-outs	Time = the chance for government to set up system of law and order
	Highway robberies	

3

What do I Know?

Once you have revised this topic thoroughly you should be able to answer most of these questions without using your notes. How many can you get right?

1 Name one town where law and order was particularly bad.
2 Which famous sheriff was sacked for 'disturbing the peace'?
3 Name the famous bank-robber brothers who specialised in train robberies.
4 What type of courts were set up to deal with problems in local towns?
5 Name the county and state where homesteaders and cattlemen went to war.
6 Who was the prostitute who was wrongly hanged by a vigilante group which accused her of cattle rustling?
7 Apart from cattle rustling what else made the cattlemen unhappy with the homesteaders?
8 Give two problems with vigilante groups.
9 Give two reasons for the lack of law and order.
10 Name two things that meant that law and order gradually improved.

My score........

Explain why these points are important in the history of law and order on the Plains:

- Barbed wire
- Vigilance committees
- Small towns, wide apart from each other
- Miners courts.

4

Exam Type Questions

There are lots of questions that could be asked about law and order. Here are a few of the main ones. Check that you can answer each one by planning it out. You could start by brainstorming the answers and then write them out to make sure that you are:

- Answering what the question is asking
- Looking for key words to focus on in the question
- Explaining your ideas
- Adding specific information and examples as proof
- Arguing (with proof) as well as just describing.

---

1 How successful was the system of law and order before 1890?

2 The settlers and the ranchers both wanted to make a success of their life on the Plains. Why then did they cause so many problems of law and order?

3 Who caused most problems on the Plains: the Indians, the cattlemen or the homesteaders?

The Struggle for the Plains

1

Topic Summary

This section covers the actual events and stages in the Plains conflict between the Indians and the white settlers. We have seen how the Indians and whites had different beliefs and how so many groups either travelled through the Plains or settled on them. The Indian problem would only get bigger. The government changed its policy as the pressure for land increased. The Indians were given land 'permanently', then the size of that land was made smaller. Finally they were forced to move onto reservations, which were so small that it was impossible to live their traditional nomadic lifestyle. Key events in the conflict were the Fort Laramie Treaty, Sand Creek Massacre, the Battle of Little Big Horn and the Battle of Wounded Knee.

2

What do I Need to Know?

You need to know the different stages of government policy and how the government decided to solve the 'Indian problem' over the period. You need to know why each stage did not really work and what key conflicts acted as turning points along the way. You also need to revise what life was like for the Indians on the reservations and what their future held.

The Permanent Indian Frontier and the Plains Wars

- In 1832 the Department of Indian Affairs in Washington agreed that the 'Great American Desert' to the west of the Mississippi river was to become the 'Permanent Indian Frontier'. Nations of Eastern Indians had already been moved leading up to this date and the future for them seemed more settled from now on.
- But in 1851 the Fort Laramie Treaty revealed that the policy had changed to 'concentrate' the Indians in a smaller protected area for which they would be paid. In return they would agree to stop attacks on government troops and travellers.
- The Plains Wars followed. The Indians were angry that the land they were given was getting smaller.
- In 1864 Chief Black Kettle went to Fort Lyon to offer to end the wars. He thought that he had an agreement from the army and would be protected. But then 450 men, women and children were massacred by Colonel Chivington. This massacre at Sand Creek led to more violence in the short term, but greater determination to find peace in the long term.

Gold and the Battle of Little Big Horn

- The next major government policy change occurred when General Custer and his men found gold in the Black Hills of Dakota. These hills were special Indian hunting grounds. But pressure increased to take this land away from the Indians and send them to reservations where they would have to settle and farm, and live like white people.
- Some Indian nations accepted this decision, but others realised it would mean the end of their lifestyle. Even chiefs who had agreed to the decision could not force every member of their tribe to follow suit.
- The government sent in the army to force remaining tribes onto the reservations. During this period General Custer was defeated by the Indians at the Battle of Little Big Horn in 1876. The public were outraged and supported the government's strict policy towards the Indians. After this many tribes surrendered.
- Custer's role in the defeat is controversial. He was a brave man but also a risk-taker who ignored orders and effectively led his men to death.

The Battle of Wounded Knee: the last battle

- The last clash between army and Indians (Sioux) was at the Battle of Wounded Knee. Here a single shot fired by an Indian, possibly by accident, led to the shooting of men, women and children. The last of the Sioux then also surrendered.
- In 1889 the government opened up the remaining areas of Indian Territory. The Oklahoma land race brought hundreds of settlers to the Plains and destroyed any remaining hopes of the Indians to save their way of life.

Summary box 1

This is a summary of why the white settlers wanted to settle on the Plains and the different methods used to remove the Indians.

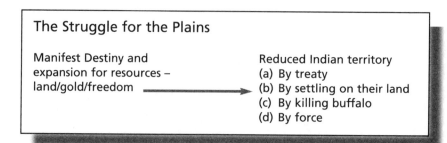

This shows that the settlement of the Great Plains seems almost inevitable when you consider the American Dream and the rising population of white people. The approach to the Indian problem was really a combination of all the methods in the diagram.

Summary box 2

This shows how government policy changed as the desire to fill the Plains grew and as other policies failed.

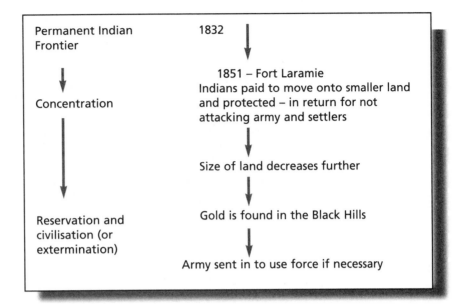

Permanent Indian Frontier	1832 ↓
↓	1851 – Fort Laramie. Indians paid to move onto smaller land and protected – in return for not attacking army and settlers
Concentration	↓
	Size of land decreases further
↓	↓
	Gold is found in the Black Hills
Reservation and civilisation (or extermination)	↓
	Army sent in to use force if necessary

3

What do I Know?

Once you have revised this topic thoroughly you should be able to answer most of these questions without using your notes. How many can you get right?

Explain the importance of these events in the history of the Plains:

- The Battle of Wounded Knee
- The army finding gold in the Black Hills of Dakota
- The Battle of Little Big Horn
- The killing of buffalo for sport
- Sand Creek Massacre.

1 Why was winter a good time to attack the Indians?
2 What was agreed at Fort Laramie in 1851?
3 Why was the slaughter of the buffalo such a powerful weapon against the Indians?
4 Give two problems with living on the reservations for an Indian.
5 Give one reason why the Indians fought with such determination at Little Big Horn.
6 Give two reasons why Custer may have been to blame for the defeat of the army.
7 Give two reasons why Custer may not have been responsible.
8 Which Indian nation held out longest against the army on the Plains?
9 What was Ghost Dancing?
10 What happened at the Battle of Wounded Knee?

My score……..

4 Using the Source

▲ **The rush for land in Oklahoma.**

What does this painting tell us about the settlers and the government at the time? (**Hint**: remember to consider whether the source gives you a true reflection of the situation at the time.)

5 Conclusion Tasks

1 Copy this chart onto a large piece of paper and fill it in to compare each group.
2 Make a list of any key similarities and differences between the different groups.
3 Include as many details and key words as you can.

Comparison Chart – Groups on the Plains				
Group and aims	**Why go to (or through) the Plains? Push and Pull factors**	**Problems – what did they have to deal with?**	**Solutions – how did they survive?**	**Contact with Indians and impact on the Plains**
Mountain men Miners Pioneers				
Mormons				
Cattlemen and cowboys				
Homesteaders				

6

Exam Type Questions

Here is the sort of question that you might find on your exam paper. See how it has been answered and assessed before you answer it yourself.

> The Indians only lost their struggle for the Plains because they were outnumbered by the cavalry who also had much better weapons. Do you agree? **(8 marks)**

Hints for your answer
- What is the question asking? Translate it for yourself, e.g. Why did the Indians lose the battle for their freedom?
- Remember to explain each idea you have.
- And add exact details as evidence.

Answer

The Indians were outnumbered by white Americans and the army had more resources and weapons to use in battles. However, the Indians also began to use rifles that they had traded, so they were not completely unmatched. In some battles the Indians actually outnumbered the cavalry, for example in the Battle of Little Big Horn where Custer and his men were defeated. So I only partly agree with the question. There must have been other reasons for their defeat.

Examiner's Comments on Answer

This student has thought about the question and has used a little detail as evidence, but has not considered any other reason why the Indians eventually lost their struggle for the Plains and moved onto reservations. I would give this answer about 3 or 4 marks out of 8.

What other factors were important in deciding the fate of the Indians? What about Manifest Destiny and the railroads, both of which encouraged people to move onto the Plains and so disrupt the Indians. Also, remember the deliberate slaughter of the buffalo which gave the Indians little choice but to rely on handouts on the reservations. You should be able to explain the ultimate clash of ideas and cultures that stood between the Indians and the whites. Remember that there are usually several factors that need explaining in a question like this and never just the examples given to you in the question itself.

Germany, 1919–45

Depth Study: Summary

This depth study focuses on the re-emergence of Germany as a major power following its defeat in the First World War. It examines in depth:

- Germany in the immediate post-war period and the problems faced by the newly created Weimar Republic.
- The rise of the Nazi Party and the reasons for the emergence of Adolf Hitler as the leader of Germany.
- The transformation of Germany from a democratic republic to a totalitarian dictatorship under the Nazis.
- The effect of Nazi rule on German life and the methods by which Nazi orthodoxy was enforced.
- The impact of the Second World War on German civilians and on attitudes towards Hitler. (The study does not, however, include an in-depth coverage of the military events of the Second World War.)

Throughout your study of this topic you will need to keep in mind three key questions about Germany in this period:

1 Why did the Weimar Republic fail?

2 Why and how did the Nazis win control of Germany?

3 How did the Nazis maintain themselves in power in the period 1933–45?

When you can provide a detailed answer to each of these three questions, you will be a long way towards being ready for the examination!

Germany under the Weimar Republic, 1919–33

....1.......................................

Topic Summary

The Weimar Republic was formed after the abdication of the Kaiser in 1918. It was a democratic government which faced serious problems in the years 1919-23. The Republic also had to carry the stigma of signing the humiliating Treaty of Versailles.

Its best years were from 1924 to 1929, but it was unable to deal with the effects of the Wall Street Crash, and Adolf Hitler and the Nazis seized power in January 1933.

....2.......................................

What do I Need to Know?

- You will need to know about the in-built weaknesses of the Weimar Republic, how the Nazi Party started and the early attempts to overthrow the Republic.
- You should also know about the policies of Gustav Stresemann and the relative stability of 1924-9.
- Finally, you should learn about the effects of Wall Street, the collapse of democratic government after 1930 and how Hitler was able to get into power.

Founding of the Weimar Republic

By October 1918 Germany was on the verge of defeat in the First World War. On 9 November Kaiser Wilhelm II abdicated and fled to Holland. On the same day Germany was declared a democratic republic. The new government was called the Weimar Republic after the town where it held its first meetings in 1919.

A Constitution (list of rules) was drawn up and published in July 1919.

- The head of state was the President, elected every seven years.
- The President appointed the Chancellor (prime-minister).
- Men and women, aged twenty and over, could vote for deputies to represent them in the Reichstag (parliament).
- The voting was based on proportional representation (PR). Parties received the same proportion of seats in parliament as they received in votes.
- If necessary the President could suspend democracy and rule by emergency decree (Article 48 of the Constitution).

Phase one: early problems, 1919–23

Weaknesses of the Weimar Republic

- The system of PR meant it was difficult for one party to win an overall majority of seats. So governments could only be made up by parties forming coalitions. This worked when times were prosperous, but it was a recipe for disaster if times were difficult.
- A number of conservative groups in Germany (including the army) were not keen on democracy. They thought it was better to have one person in control, as the Kaiser had been before the War.

Parties of the Weimar Republic
Communist Party
Social Democratic Party
Democratic Party
Centre Party
People's Party
National Party
Nazi Party

Political problems

Straight away the Weimar Republic had difficulties.

- Representatives of the Republic signed the armistice to end the War on 11 November 1918 and the Treaty of Versailles in July 1919. The belief grew up in Germany that the army could have fought on, but they were 'stabbed in the back' by the politicians. Some people called the politicians the 'November Criminals'. The treaty was widely resented and people never forgot that Weimar politicians agreed to such a humiliating treaty.

There were three early attempts to overthrow the Weimar Republic:

- The Spartacist Rising of January 1919. The Spartacists, led by Rosa Luxemburg and Karl Liebknecht, were crushed by the army.
- The Kapp Putsch of March 1920. A group of right wing nationalists, led by Wolfgang Kapp, tried to take control of Berlin. They failed and Kapp fled the country.
- The Munich Putsch of November 1923. Adolf Hitler and the Nazis tried to gain control of Munich, but they were arrested by police.

Economic problems

- Germany was left exhausted by the war and the Treaty of Versailles took away some of its raw materials. German industry's ability to make and sell goods was reduced.
- In 1921 reparation payments of £6,600 million was fixed. The Weimar government printed more money and inflation set in.
- In January 1923 Germany missed a reparation payment and French troops invaded and occupied the Ruhr. German workers went on strike and production fell. The government printed even more money and the mark became worthless. Hyperinflation reduced the value of people's savings and some people were ruined. They blamed the Weimar government and so it became increasingly unpopular.

Summary box 1

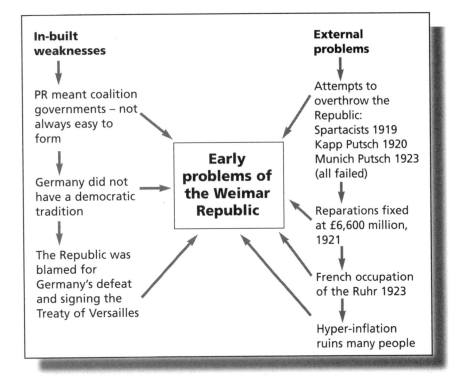

Phase two: the Golden Age of Weimar, 1924–9

In 1923 Gustav Stresemann of the German People's Party became Chancellor of Germany. He was then the Foreign Minister until 1929. He brought in a period of prosperity and good relations with foreign countries.

Economic recovery

- Stresemann stabilised the economy by introducing a new currency – the rentenmark. He also called off the strikes in the Ruhr. These measures helped to bring the hyper-inflation to an end.
- In 1924 Stresemann agreed to the Dawes Plan. The USA agreed to loan money to Germany, and more realistic targets for the payment of reparations were set. German industry benefited from American investment and, by 1929, was producing a third more goods than in 1913. The deadline for reparations was extended to 1988 in the Young Plan of 1929.

Improved relations with other countries

- Stresemann signed the Locarno Pact (1925) and the Kellogg-Briand Pact (1928). This led to other countries starting to show more trust in Germany and in 1926 Germany was allowed to join the League of Nations.

Political stability

- The improved economy and better relations with other countries helped to make the Weimar Republic more stable and coalitions held together more successfully.
- With Germany doing well, very few people were interested in supporting the extremist parties such as the Communists and the Nazis. Both did badly in Reichstag elections.

The revival of art and culture

- The Stresemann years were also good for German art and culture, which underwent a revival. Some things to mention are the paintings of George Grosz and the architecture of Walter Gropius' Bauhaus movement.

Note

> Some historians believe that the 'golden age' was an illusion. Underneath the apparent stability, weaknesses remained.
>
> - Germany's economic prosperity was based on foreign loans. Exports were falling and the welfare programme was expensive.
> - Many Germans felt that Stresemann had been too cautious in dealing with other countries. They wanted reparations scrapped and the Treaty of Versailles reversed.
> - Political stability was still in question. Many politicians were self-centred and failed to realise that a successful democracy needed people to compromise.
>
> These weaknesses help explain why in 1929 the Weimar Republic was incapable of dealing with the depression and the emergence of Hitler and a well-organised Nazi Party.

Summary box 2

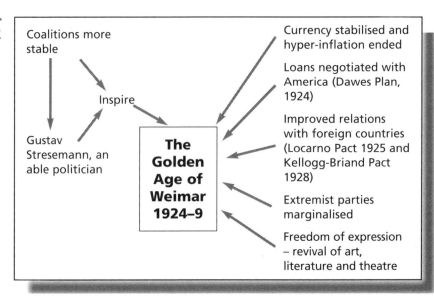

Coalitions more stable

Gustav Stresemann, an able politician

Inspire

The Golden Age of Weimar 1924–9

Currency stabilised and hyper-inflation ended

Loans negotiated with America (Dawes Plan, 1924)

Improved relations with foreign countries (Locarno Pact 1925 and Kellogg-Briand Pact 1928)

Extremist parties marginalised

Freedom of expression – revival of art, literature and theatre

...*3*....................................

What do I Know

Once you have revised this topic thoroughly you should be able to answer most of these questions without using your notes. How many can you get right?

---

1 Why was Germany's new Constitution called the Weimar Republic?
2 Name the two presidents of the Weimar Republic.
3 Who was allowed to vote in elections to the Reichstag?
4 What was Article 48?
5 Give one reason why the Weimar Republic was disliked by many from the start.
6 Who tried to overthrow the Republic in 1923?
7 What were reparations set at in 1921?
8 What two positions in the Weimar government did Gustav Stresemann hold?
9 Name one agreement Stresemann made with other countries.
10 Give an example of German art and culture thriving in the 1920s.

My score ....

Explain the importance of the following in the history of Germany:

- The Weimar Constitution
- The Treaty of Versailles
- Gustav Stresemann.

...*4*....................................

Exam Type Questions

Here are examples of questions which you might be asked in an examination, together with students' answers and examiner's comments. Read the answers carefully and see what the examiner has to say about them.

Study the cartoon and then answer the questions.

" PERHAPS IT WOULD GEE-UP BETTER IF WE LET IT TOUCH EARTH "

▲ This cartoon appeared in a British newspaper. The characters shown are Aristide Briand, the Premier of France, and David Lloyd-George, the Prime Minister of Britain.

1 Briefly describe the terms of the Treaty of Versailles and why it was disliked by the German people. **(6 marks)**

2 What is the message of the cartoon? **(6 marks)**

3 How useful is the source for historians studying the problems of the Weimar Republic? **(8 marks)**

Question 1: Answer

The Treaty of Versailles was very harsh on Germany. It lost territory in Germany, such as Alsace Lorraine, to France and West Prussia and Posen to Poland. Germany also lost all her colonies. Germany's army was limited to 100,000 and no troops were allowed inside the Rhineland. On top of this Germany had to accept the blame for starting the war (war-guilt) and was made to pay war damages (reparations). The treaty was so disliked because it was a humiliation for the German people. The treaty had been dictated – the Germans were not allowed to negotiate the terms. There was no give and take at all – Germany was severely punished. The treaty stuck in the throats of the Germans and it was the Weimar government which got the blame. The treaty hung like a millstone around the necks of the Weimar politicians. Not only did it help to bring down Weimar in 1933, but it could also be seen as a long-term cause of the Second World War.

Question 2: Answer

This cartoon is about the payment of reparations. The Treaty of Versailles laid down that reparations had to be paid by Germany, but the amount was not fixed until 1921. Germany was ordered to pay £6,600 million, a ridiculous amount. The cartoonist clearly thinks this is too much because the horse (Germany) cannot pull the 'indemnity' cart. It is so heavy the horse has been lifted off the ground. Briand is shown holding the whip and rein because it was France who wanted to give Germany a good thrashing as revenge for the war. Lloyd-George is shown in a rather pathetic pose. I think this was because he probably thought the reparations were too much but did not dare say it in public – he would have lost votes!

Low was probably right. German industry had been ruined by the war and the Treaty of Versailles had taken iron ore and coal away. No wonder the impression is given that the amount of reparations is holding back Germany's recovery.

**Question 3:
Answer**

This source does have some uses but, on its own, has some limitations as evidence about the problems of the Weimar Republic. The cartoon informs us that people at the time could see the reparations were too high and that Germany was going to have problems paying them. From this it is possible to infer that reparations would have been unpopular and therefore a problem for the Weimar government. The source, however, tells us nothing about the other problems facing Weimar – constitutional weaknesses, the lack of a democratic tradition in Germany, the attempts to overthrow it and so on.

**Question 1:
Examiner's
Comments on
Answer**

I think this is probably worth full marks. The student has a good grasp of the terms of the Treaty of Versailles and appreciates the reasons why it was hated.

I particularly like the way the answer links the unpopularity of the treaty to the failure of the Weimar Republic. One point to note here is that only six marks have been allocated to this question. I have the feeling this student could have written more, but more time spent answering here would have meant less time on the other questions. Good technique, in sharing out time in proportion to the marks available, has been demonstrated by the student.

**Question 2:
Examiner's
Comments on
Answer**

I like this answer. The student has shown good interpretative skills and put the cartoon into the context of the times. The student has seen that the cartoon is linked directly to the Treaty of Versailles and has shown excellent background knowledge. The direct references to the horse and cart, Briand and Lloyd-George are placed into the context of attitudes and viewpoints held at the time. There is also a subtle comment about the accuracy of the cartoonist's view. A very good answer. Again I would probably give full marks.

**Question 3:
Examiner's
Comments on
Answer**

The student has approached the question in the right way, noting that it is asking 'How useful?' Therefore, both uses and limitations have to be considered. The answer sees that the reparation payments would be a problem for the Republic, but does not tell us anything about the other problems. Thus, its usefulness is limited. The answer could have enlarged on the nature of the other problems and commented on whether the source would give a typical picture. It is a British source – German sources would probably have been even more damning about the amount of reparations to be paid. As the answer has not considered how typical the image given is, or mentioned that the source tells us about British attitudes at the time (as reflected in this cartoon in a newspaper), I would give this 5 out of 8.

The Rise of Hitler and the Fall of the Weimar Republic, 1929–33

1

Topic Summary

By mid-1929 Germany was prospering once more. Political stability had been resolved and relations with other countries had improved dramatically. By the end of the year, however, things had begun to go wrong. The talented Gustav Stresemann died in October and in the same month the Wall Sreet Crash brought down the American economy. Since German recovery had been based upon American loans the German people suffered too. As the government failed to deal with the new economic problems support for the Nazis grew. Finally, in January 1933, Hitler became Chancellor.

2

What do I Need to Know?

The examiners will expect you to be able to explain how things went so badly wrong for the Weimar Republic. You will need to show how a government which seemed to be doing so well in mid-1929 fell apart and how the Nazi Party (which had very little support in 1928) came to be the major political force in Germany.

The origins of the Nazi Party

- In January 1919 Anton Drexler formed the German Workers' Party (DAP). Adolf Hitler joined the DAP in September 1919. Hitler had fought in the First World War and was violently opposed to both the Treaty of Versailles and the Weimar Republic.
- In 1920 the DAP was renamed the National Socialist German Workers' Party or NSDAP (Nazi for short). Its beliefs were published in its Twenty-Five Point Programme. In July 1921, Hitler became the leader.
- In October 1921 the *Sturm Abteilung* (SA) was formed. Also known as Stormtroopers or Brownshirts, they were set up to protect Nazi meetings and beat up political opponents.

The Munich Putsch, 8–9 November 1923

- By 1923 the Weimar Republic was faced with hyper-inflation and the French occupation of the Ruhr (see page 114). Hitler thought the Republic was on the verge of collapse and decided to try to seize power.

- On 8 November 1923, Hitler declared a 'national revolution' and the next day 3,000 members of the SA marched through the centre of Munich. The police opened fire and killed 16 marchers.
- Hitler was arrested and put on trial. He was sentenced to five year's imprisonment. Hitler used the trial to criticise the Republic and put forward his own ideas about Germany's future.

Hitler reforms the Nazi Party

- Hitler only served nine months of his sentence. While in prison he wrote *Mein Kampf* ('My Struggle') telling his life-story and setting out his beliefs.

Hitler's beliefs

Among other things Hitler said:

- the Treaty of Versailles should be destroyed
- the Germans (or Aryans) were the master race
- the German people needed extra territory or living space (*lebensraum*)
- the Jews were an inferior race and responsible for Germany's problems
- there was no place for democracy in Germany. The country should be run by one strong leader who had to obeyed (the Fuhrer).

- When Hitler came out of prison in December 1924, the fortunes of the Weimar Republic were improving and few people had any time for extremists such as the Nazis.
- Hitler realised that the Nazi Party needed to be better organised and that power had to be won through elections. Using force would not work.
- Between 1924 and 1928 he reorganised the Nazi Party and strengthened his own position as leader. Despite this the Nazi Party only won 12 seats in the 1928 election.

Hitler comes to power, 1929–33

1 Economic crisis: the Wall Street Crash, 1929

- Stresemann died on 3 October 1929. The Weimar Republic had lost one of its most able politicians.
- On 29 October 1929 the Wall Street Crash shook the world. Share prices hit rock bottom on the New York stock exchange and businesses went bankrupt overnight.
- The American banks called in the loans they had made to Germany. German industry could not operate. Factories closed and by 1932 there were six million people unemployed. Germany was in economic depression and the memories of 1923 returned. Once again the Weimar government was blamed.

2 Political crisis: rule by decree

The economic crisis led to a political crisis in Germany.

- The parties in the grand coalition of the time could not agree on how to tackle the economic depression. They argued about whether unemployment benefit should be reduced or not. The government fell apart and, in March 1930, Chancellor Muller resigned and was replaced by Heinrich Bruning.
- Hitler exploited the economic crisis to win support for the Nazi Party. He toured Germany and made numerous speeches blaming weak government for Germany's problems. Mass rallies were held and propaganda leaflets and posters were published. The SA was used to threaten political opponents.
- The economic depression hit all sections of German society and people listened to Hitler's message. He told them that he would provide strong leadership and restore economic prosperity and full employment. And that he would protect big business and industry from the Communists.

Many were attracted to his arguments, including industrialists such as Fritz Thyssen. Alfred Hugenberg, leader of the Germany National Party (DNVP) and a newspaper owner, allowed Hitler to publish his policies in his newspapers.

- In the elections of September 1930 the Nazis won 107 seats and the Communists 77. People were clearly losing faith in democracy and the Weimar Republic.
- After the election, Bruning was unable to form a coalition government. So he ruled by emergency decrees signed by President Hindenburg. Parliamentary democracy had been replaced by a semi-dictatorship. The Reichstag met less and less frequently.

3 Hitler becomes Chancellor, 1933

- In April 1932 Hitler ran for president. Hindenburg was voted back in with 19 million votes but Hitler received a massive 13 million votes.
- Bruning resigned in May 1932. He was replaced by Franz von Papen.
- In the elections of July 1932 the Nazis won 230 seats and became the largest single party in the Reichstag.
- In November 1932 another election was held. Although the Nazi vote fell to 196 seats, they were still the biggest party in the Reichstag and had every right to be part of the government. Hitler, however, said that the Nazis would not enter any coalition unless he was made Chancellor. Hindenburg refused.
- But Papen lacked support and made a deal with Hitler, proposing a new government with Hitler as Chancellor and himself as Vice-Chancellor. Hindenburg agreed. Papen mistakenly thought he would be able to get rid of Hitler later.
- Hitler was made Chancellor on 30 January 1933. He had achieved his aim of getting into power legally.

Summary box

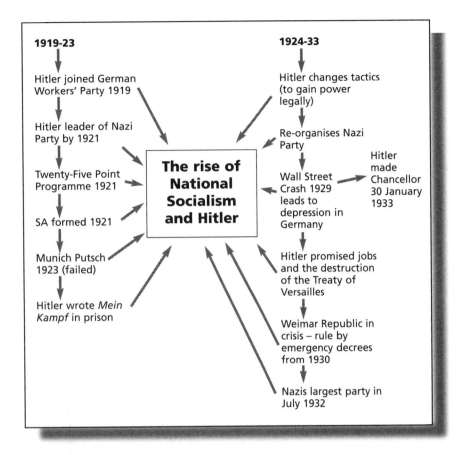

1919-23

Hitler joined German Workers' Party 1919

Hitler leader of Nazi Party by 1921

Twenty-Five Point Programme 1921

SA formed 1921

Munich Putsch 1923 (failed)

Hitler wrote *Mein Kampf* in prison

The rise of National Socialism and Hitler

1924-33

Hitler changes tactics (to gain power legally)

Re-organises Nazi Party

Wall Street Crash 1929 leads to depression in Germany

Hitler made Chancellor 30 January 1933

Hitler promised jobs and the destruction of the Treaty of Versailles

Weimar Republic in crisis – rule by emergency decrees from 1930

Nazis largest party in July 1932

3

What do I Know

Once you have revised this topic thoroughly you should be able to answer most of these questions without using your notes. How many can you get right?

Explain the importance of the following in the history of Germany:

- The failure of the Munich Putsch
- *Mein Kampf*
- Economic depression after 1929
- Hitler's personality.

1 Who started the German Workers' Party?
2 What new name did this party adopt in 1920?
3 Which document set out its policies?
4 What was the SA?
5 What was *Mein Kampf*?
6 Why did the Nazis change their tactics after 1924?
7 How many seats did the Nazis win in the 1928 election?
8 Which two parties won increased support in the Reichstag elections as a result of economic depression in Germany?
9 How many seats did the Nazis win in July 1932?
10 When did Hitler become Chancellor?

My score........

4

Exam Type Questions

Here is a common question set in exams on Nazi Germany, together with a student answer and an examiner's comments on it. Read the answer carefully and see what the examiner has to say about it.

> Why did Hitler and the Nazis come to power in 1933?
>
> **(15 marks)**

Answer

Hitler was able to come to power in 1933 because of the internal weaknesses of the Weimar Republic and the crisis brought about by the Wall Street Crash which plunged Germany into an economic depression. Linked to this was Hitler's determination, the slick propaganda machine of the Nazis and the ruthlessness of the SA in intimidating opponents. What is more Hitler achieved power through legal means.

The Weimar constitution was very democratic. Voting was by proportional representation, which meant that even minority parties could win seats in the Reichstag (German parliament). However, this also meant that governments were based on coalitions – a potential weakness in the absence of any compromise. The Constitution also allowed the President to rule by decree in times of crisis (Article 48). Although, this was meant to be a way of protecting democracy, Article 48 was used to destroy the Republic between 1930 and 1933. Coupled with this was the fact that the Weimar Republic was blamed for signing the Treaty of Versailles and the hyper-inflation of 1923. Both these things were never forgotten by the German people. They lay under the surface for a bit but came back to haunt the Republic after 1929.

Hitler tried to seize power in 1923 (the Munich Putsch) but failed. The Nazis were far too weak in 1923, but the failure of the putsch made Hitler see that violence was counter-productive. In future the Nazis would concentrate on legal methods. The next four years were spent reorganising the party, streamlining the Nazi message and devising ways of putting it over to the public. Despite this there was no way Hitler was going to win power between 1924 and 1929, the years of Stresemann. These were relatively good years and very few were interested in extremist parties

Then, came a turning point – the Wall Street Crash of 1929 plunged Germany into economic depression. Unemployment rose to six million by 1932. The Weimar government seemed unable to cope with the effects of the Depression. Politicians started to bicker and saw the Depression as a chance to further their own ambitions –

> rather than to work together for the good of Germany. After 1930 rule by decree was used more and more. Hitler began to say things the German people warmed to. He said he would end unemployment and rid Germany of the Treaty of Versailles. His speeches were dramatic and he was backed by the exciting ceremonial of Nazi rallies. People began to think this man was the answer. In July 1932 the Nazis became the biggest party in the Reichstag (230 seats) and Hitler made his claim for power.
>
> He was made Chancellor on 30 January 1933. His rise had been a combination of the weaknesses of Weimar, the economic depression and his own personal qualities. But out of them I would say it was the weaknesses of the Republic which was the most important. If it had not been Hitler it would have been someone else.

Examiner's Comments

This is a very strong answer. I would award this at least 13 marks. The student has a good technique for extended answers. First, a summary of the answer is given at the beginning and the rest of the answer provides evidence to support this. There are places where the student could have said a little more. There is, for example, little said about which people supported Hitler. Perhaps it might have made more attempt to weigh up the relative importance of the individual causes.

The student has tried to be analytical and there is some attempt to link the causes for Hitler's rise together. This is backed up by clear, accurate factual support. I also like the references to the way that Hitler turned the failure of the Munich Putsch into an advantage.

Remember to give as much supporting detail in your answers as possible.

5

Practice Questions

Now let's see what you can do. Study the cartoon on page 126 and then answer the questions.

---

1 Describe the political events in Germany between July 1932 and January 1933. **(6 marks)**

2 What is the message of the cartoon? **(6 marks)**

3 How useful is the source for historians studying Hitler's rise to power? **(8 marks)**

4 What problems faced the Weimar Republic in 1919-23? **(10 marks)**

5 How did the Republic overcome these problems? **(10 marks)**

▲ This cartoon appeared in *Vorwarts,* the newspaper of the Social Democrat Party, on 1 February 1933. The cartoon is called 'Hugenberg's Driving School'. Hugenberg is saying to Papen: 'That newcomer up there in front can imagine all he wants that he's steering but we'll set the economic course!'

Hints for success

- In question 1 try to make your answers concise, but detached.
- In question 2 remember to comment on things in the cartoon to support your answer.
- In question 3 don't forget that 'How useful' also means that you have to look at the ways that the source is not useful.
- In question 4 do not just list the problems of the Republic. Try to show how they were linked together and make some comment about which problem you think was the most serious.
- In question 5 you should refer to the work of Stresemann and the failure of the Munich Putsch.
- The best answers, however, will note that the problems were only overcome temporarily. The constitutional problems and being linked with the Treaty of Versailles were still there.

The Rise and Fall of the Weimar Republic

1 Here is a list of the some of the main events in the history of the Weimar Republic. Place the correct number (or numbers) in the space beside the relevant date on the graph. Then write an explanation of what the graph shows and you have the making of an essay on the history of the Weimar Republic.

EVENT	No	EVENT	No
• The Weimar Republic was proclaimed.	1	• The Spartacists tried to overthrow the Republic.	9
• Wolfgang Kapp tried to overthrow the Republic.	2	• The Allies said that Germany would have to pay £6,600 million in reparations.	10
• High inflation in Germany.	3	• The Dawes Plan.	11
• The Munich Putsch.	4	• Germany joined the League of Nations.	12
• The Locarno Pact.	5	• Wall Street Crash.	13
• The Kellogg-Briand Pact.	6	• USA said it would not lend any more money to Germany. German industry collapsed.	14
• Hindenburg started to rule by decree.	7		
• Treaty of Versailles signed.	8	• Adolf Hitler became Chancellor.	15

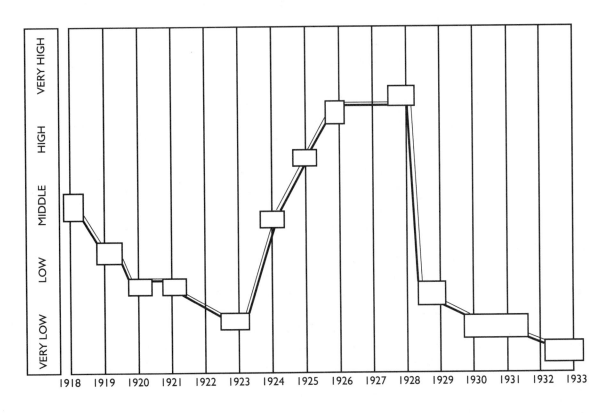

From Democracy to Dictatorship, 1933–4

········1·······················

Topic Summary

After Hitler became Chancellor in 1933, he set about making Germany a totalitarian dictatorship – a one-party state which controlled all aspects of people's lives. Hitler used propaganda and terror to control the German population. He instituted a racial policy which led to the persecution of the Jews and other minority groups. The German economy was geared towards preparing for war, which broke out in 1939. After 1941, opposition and resistance to Hitler grew. He committed suicide in April 1945.

········2·······················

What do I Need to Know?

You will need to know how Hitler made Germany a dictatorship between 1933 and 1934, the nature of the totalitarian state (propaganda methods, removal of individual freedoms and use of terror).

You also need to know about Nazi racial policies, economic policies, attitudes to art and culture, and the role of women. Finally, you need to have knowledge of opposition and resistance to Hitler.

Between 1933 and 1934 Adolf Hitler turned Germany into a dictatorship. He skilfully used the Weimar Constitution to do this – the so-called 'legal revolution'.

- After becoming Chancellor, Hitler persuaded President Hindenburg to call an election for 5 March 1933. Hitler wanted the Nazis to have an overall majority in the Reichstag.
- On 27 February 1933 the Reichstag buildings were burned to the ground. Marinus van der Lubbe, a Dutch communist, was blamed but the fire may well have been started by the Nazis. Hindenburg agreed to invoke Article 48, which allowed Hitler to have emergency powers in a 'time of crisis'. Hitler used these powers to control other political parties.
- The Nazis won 288 seats, less than half – Hitler needed a two-thirds majority before he could legally make changes he wanted to the Constitution. Hitler achieved the necessary majority by using his emergency powers to stop the Communists from taking their 81 seats. He also got the Centre Party to support him by saying he would not harm the Catholic religion. For good measure, the SA surrounded the building to intimidate any would-be opponents.

- The Enabling Act was passed by 444 votes to 94 votes, with only the Social Democrats voting against it. This gave the government the power to pass laws without consulting the Reichstag. In July 1933 the Enabling Act was used to ban all other political parties, making Germany a one-party state.
- Hitler needed the support of the German army. To keep this, on 30 June 1934 Hitler had the leaders of the SA (including Rohm) murdered by the SS. The event became known as the 'Night of the Long Knives'.
- President Hindenburg died on 2 August 1934. Hitler now united the positions of Chancellor and President and declared himself the Fuhrer of Germany. The army swore an oath of loyalty to Hitler (not Germany!). The Weimar Republic and democracy was dead and buried.

Summary box 1

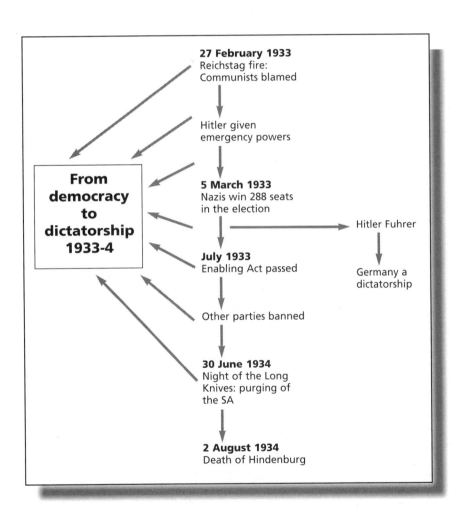

How the Nazis controlled the German people

The Nazis used propaganda, censorship and terror to consolidate their power and control the German people, thus making Germany a totalitarian state under the dictatorship of one person.

1 Propaganda and censorship

- In 1933 the Ministry for People's Enlightenment and Propaganda was set up under Josef Goebbels. It controlled the radio, press and all areas of culture (films, literature, art and the theatre). 'Degenerate' (non-Nazi) books were burned and school textbooks rewritten to reflect Nazi ideas.
- Huge Nazi Party rallies and processions were organised to impress the German people.
- Posters, photographs of Hitler and swastika flags went on display throughout Germany. Hitler was shown as a strong, confident leader.
- The Olympic Games, held in Berlin in 1936, was used to promote a positive image of Nazism.

2 Terror

- The *Schutzstaffel* (SS) was formed in 1925 as the elite bodyguard of the Nazi leaders. From 1929 its leader was Heinrich Himmler. From 1934 the SS controlled the concentration camps and from 1936 the Gestapo (secret police) was brought under the control of the SS. The SS and Gestapo were ruthless in seeking out any opposition to the Nazis.
- From 1933 concentration camps were set up. They were originally used to detain political prisoners and people whom the Nazis regarded as 'undesirable' (gypsies, Jews and homosexuals). Remember it was not until later, during the Second World War, that many concentration camps became death camps.
- In 1934 the People's Court was set up under Judge Roland Freisler to try people who opposed the Nazi regime.

Summary box 2

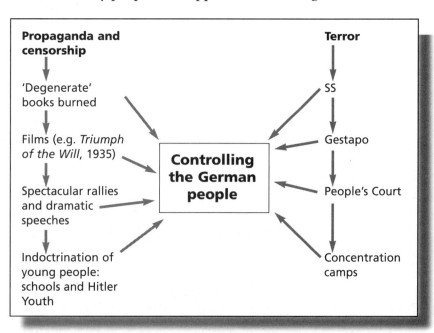

Propaganda and censorship

'Degenerate' books burned

Films (e.g. *Triumph of the Will*, 1935)

Spectacular rallies and dramatic speeches

Indoctrination of young people: schools and Hitler Youth

Controlling the German people

Terror

SS

Gestapo

People's Court

Concentration camps

3

What do I Know?

Once you have revised this topic thoroughly you should be able to answer most of these questions without using your notes. How many can you get right?

1 What is a totalitarian dictatorship?
2 Why did Hitler want an election in March 1933?
3 What happened on 27 February 1933?
4 How did Hitler secure a two-third's majority after the election?
5 What was the Enabling Act?
6 Why did Hitler murder the leaders of the SA?
7 What happened on 2 August 1934?
8 Who was head of the Ministry for People's Enlightenment and Propaganda?
9 What methods of propaganda did the Nazis use to influence the German people?
10 What methods did the Nazis use to terrorise the German people into following Nazism?

My score........

Explain the importance of the following in the history of Germany:

- The Enabling Act
- Nazi propaganda
- The SS.

4

Exam Type Questions

Here are two examples of questions which you might be asked in an examination, together with students' answers and examiner's comments. Study Sources A and B, read the answers carefully and then see what the examiner thought of them.

1 Why did Hitler blame the Communists for the Reichstag fire?
(10 marks)

2 Why was the Enabling Act important in making Germany a dictatorship?
(10 marks)

Source A

◀ **The Reichstag buildings on fire, 27 February 1933.**

Source B

> The Reichstag has passed the following law:
>
> In addition to the procedure outlined for the passing of Acts in the Constitution, the [Nazi] government is also able to pass laws.
>
> The laws passed by the government will be announced by the Chancellor [Adolf Hitler].

▲ **Taken from the Enabling Act, passed on 23 March 1933.**

Question 1: Answers

Student A

The Communists were a danger to the Nazis winning an overall majority in the election which was to take place on 5 March 1933. The Nazis were right wing and the Communists were left wing. Hitler had promised the industrialists that he would protect them from the Communists. If the Communists got into power they would take factories away from the bosses and give them to the government.

Student B

There is no definite truth that the Communists did burn down the Reichstag. Some historians believe that the Nazis started the fire themselves. There were members of the SA in the vicinity of the Reichstag on 27 February. A Dutch communist, Marinus van der Lubbe, was found on the scene and arrested for arson.
The point is the Nazis exploited the fire to discredit the Communist Party in Germany. An election was due on 5 March 1933 and Hitler wanted to put people off from voting for the Communists. He was afraid that they would stop the Nazis getting the overall majority of seats they needed to change the constitution. The Communists were an extreme left-wing party and, like the Nazis, had been on the up in recent Reichstag elections. The day after the fire President Hindenburg was persuaded to pass an emergency decree to 'protect the people and state'. This was used by the Nazis to whip up anti-Communist feeling. There was a lot of intimidation by the SA on the streets. Hundreds of Communists were arrested. The fire was an ideal chance to give the Communists a bad name.

Question 2: Answers

Student A

The Enabling Act meant that Hitler could rule Germany and pass laws on his own. He no longer needed to consult the deputies in the Reichstag. It gave him the power to do things which strengthened his own position at the expense of the other parties. The Act was part of the Nazi's legal revolution. They had used the Constitution to get the Act passed.

Student B

The Enabling Act was a big step forward in the Nazi's legal revolution. Hitler now had the power to pass laws (as Source B says) without debate or consultation. The deputies in the Reichstag had lost any real power.

Hitler now used the Enabling Act to get rid of his opposition. In July 1933 the Act was used to ban all political parties (other than the Nazis, of course) and then he banned the trade unions so that the workers were brought under his control. When Hindenburg died in 1934 nothing could be done by the Reichstag to stop Hitler from uniting the positions of Chancellor and President into one: Fuhrer of Germany. So the Enabling Act was a landmark in itself for Hitler, but just as important was the way he used it.

Question 1: Examiner's Comments on Answers

Student A

There are two reasons given why the Nazis wanted to discredit the Communists and some contextual support. I like the fact that the student has shown some appreciation of what the Communists stood for. I would give this 5 marks.

Student B

This is a very good answer. There is plenty of support and several reasons which the student links together. The answer is analytical and shows awareness that there is debate among historians about the fire. I would give this 9 of 10.

Question 2: Examiner's Comments on Answers

Student A

This shows some perception. More than one reason is given and there is a hint of a higher level answer when there is general mention that Hitler used the Act to do other things. However, these other things are not really mentioned. I like the contextual comment at the end about the legal revolution and the fact that Hitler was using the Constitution to destroy democracy. I would give this 5 or 6 marks.

Student B

This is a very good answer. It shows an excellent understanding of what the Act said and shows how it was used to move Germany towards totalitarianism. The supporting knowledge is exact and there is an attempt to show how the reasons linked together. I would give this 9 marks.

The Effect of Nazi Rule on German Life

...1...

Topic Summary

Hitler had quickly established himself in power and then set about spreading Nazi ideas throughout Germany. Nazism was to be a way of life in Germany with conformity expected from young and old in how they worshipped, how they were educated and what they read and listened to. In the case of the Jews, Nazi philosophy even extended to restrictions on their civil rights – and ultimately their right to live.

...2...

What do I Need to Know?

To answer questions in the exam effectively you will need to explain why Hitler persecuted the Jews and to provide details on the increasing severity of their treatment. You will also have to show how Hitler ensured that the young of the country were kept in line and how education, religion, the arts and the labour market were brought under control.

1 The Nazis and race

Hitler and the Nazis aimed to make the German people into a master race. This also involved the persecution of other groups, such as the Jews, who were considered inferior.

The master race

- Hitler gave the SS the job of purifying the German people to make them into an Aryan master race. The ideal Aryan was tall, had blond hair and blue eyes, and pure Germanic blood.
- Race farms were established. Here carefully selected women to be used for breeding children with SS officers – a policy of selective breeding.
- 'Race Studies' were introduced to indoctrinate young people with Nazi racial ideas.

Persecution of Jews

1933	SA organise boycott of Jewish shops. Jews banned from work in professions such as civil service.
1935	Jews banned from certain swimming pools, parks, cinemas etc. Nuremberg Laws removed citizens vote from Jews. Marriage and sexual relations between Jews and Aryans banned.
1938	Kristallnacht. Thousands of Jews arrested and sent to concentration camps.
1942	Jews forced to wear Star of David and confined to ghettos. Beginning of 'Final Solution'.

Other minority groups

- Other groups persecuted by the Nazis were tramps, alcoholics, homosexuals, gypsies and the mentally disabled.

2 The Nazis and religion

The Catholic Church in Germany

- In 1933 Hitler agreed a Concordat with the Pope whereby he would not meddle with the Catholic Church if it kept out of politics. In 1937, however, Hitler arrested several Catholic priests and put them into concentration camps.

The Protestant Church in Germany

The Protestant Church was split in its attitude towards the Nazis.

- Some Protestants were happy to support Nazism. They called themselves German Christians and were led by Ludwig Muller.
- Other Protestants opposed Nazism and broke away to form the Confessional Church under Martin Niemoller, who was not scared to criticise the Nazis. Hitler had him arrested and imprisoned in 1937.

The German Faith Movement

This was an attempt by the Nazis to replace Christianity with their own form of religion. Very few people joined it.

3 Education and young people

Schools and universities

Hitler believed that indoctrinating the young into the Nazi way of thinking would make the regime permanent in Germany.

- Textbooks were rewritten to give only Nazi viewpoints.
- Teachers had to join the Nazi Teachers' Association.
- Students were told of the humiliation of Versailles and how Hitler would restore Germany's greatness.
- Jews were picked on by teachers and ridiculed in class.

The Hitler Youth Movement

- The Hitler Youth catered for young people outside of school hours, but had the same purpose as the schools – indoctrination. Boys joined the Little Fellows (aged 6–10), the Young Folk (aged 10–14) and finally, from 14 to 18, they were part of Hitler Youth. Girls between 10 and 14 started off in the Young Girls (10–14) and from 14 to 17 joined the League of German Maidens.
- For boys the activities were centred on physical fitness and military-style training. The girls were taught about motherhood.

The role of women

- According to Nazi doctrine, a women's place was in the home bringing up the children. Large families were encouraged and a medal was given to mothers who had more than eight children.

- Under the Nazis women were denied jobs and excluded from the professions.
- Women were needed to work in the factories in the war. But, even so, they were paid less than men.

Nazi art and culture

The Nazis used art and culture as a propaganda tool.

- Paintings by Weimar artists, such as Paul Klee, were declared 'degenerate' and approved paintings portrayed Nazi ideals.
- Propaganda films, such as *Triumph of the Will*, celebrated the Nazi movement. Other films whipped up prejudice and hatred against Jews and communists.

Summary box

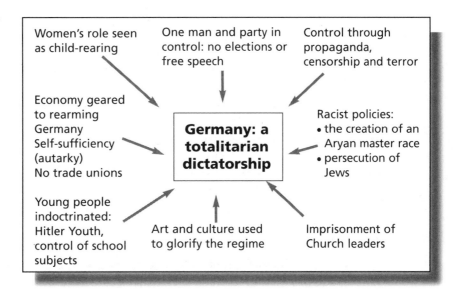

Women's role seen as child-rearing

One man and party in control: no elections or free speech

Control through propaganda, censorship and terror

Economy geared to rearming Germany
Self-sufficiency (autarky)
No trade unions

Germany: a totalitarian dictatorship

Racist policies:
- the creation of an Aryan master race
- persecution of Jews

Young people indoctrinated: Hitler Youth, control of school subjects

Art and culture used to glorify the regime

Imprisonment of Church leaders

Economic policy

- Hitler wanted the economy to prepare Germany for war. He wanted jobs for the unemployed and self-sufficiency (autarky) so that Germany would not have to rely on importing goods if there was a war.
- Dr Hjalmar Schacht was put in charge of the economy. But he was slow to get rearmament going, so Hitler sacked him.
- In 1936 Hermann Goering introduced a Four Year Plan to speed up rearmament, so that Germany was ready for war. The production of guns, tanks and aircraft was stepped up.
- Autarky was set in motion by encouraging the development of industries making synthetic materials such as plastics and nylon.
- Unemployment was reduced by building houses and motorways and recruitment into the armed forces.
- The German Labour Front, headed by Dr Robert Ley, set hours and wages and disciplined workers who broke the rules. Two other organisations, Beauty of Labour and Strength through Joy, were set up to improve conditions for workers.

- Trade unions were banned. Workers were now under the control of the state and expected to work for the good of Germany.
- The living standards of the workers, however, hardly improved. Prices rose quicker than wages and there were few household consumer goods in the shops – German factories were more geared to making heavy goods.

3

What do I Know?

Once you have revised the topic thoroughly you should be able to answer most of these questions without using your notes. How many can you get right?

Explain the importance of the following in the history of Germany:

- The Hitler Youth
- The Concordat
- The Nuremberg Laws.

---

1. What did Hitler think the ideal Aryan should look like?
2. Why were young people taught 'Race Studies'?
3. What were the Nuremberg Laws?
4. Which other groups did Hitler persecute?
5. What was the Concordat?
6. What was the Confessional Church?
7. What was the German Faith Movement?
8. How was the Hitler Youth organised?
9. What was the Nazi attitude to women?
10. According to the Nazis, what was 'degenerate' art?

My score........

4

Exam Type Questions

Here are the sorts of questions you might be asked in an exam, together with student answers and examiner's comments on them. Read the anwers carefully and then see what the examiner thought of them.

Study the sources below and then answer the questions.

---

1. How did the Nazis see the role of women? Use Sources A and B and your own knowledge in your answer. **(6 marks)**

2. Why would the Nazis have published posters such as Source A? **(7 marks)**

3. Which was more important in controlling the German people: propaganda or terror? Explain your answer. **(12 marks)**

Source A

◀ A Nazi propaganda poster. It stresses the importance of women as mothers and housewives.

Source B

'Woman has the task of being beautiful and bringing children into the world'.

A comment by Josef Goebbels, in charge of the Nazi Ministry for People's Enlightenment and Propaganda.

Question 1: Answer

The Nazis wanted the women to be housewives and have lots of children. The poster (Source A) shows a woman and child. The woman's job is to rear children. You can see a man ploughing in the background. The Nazis saw men as the breadwinners.

Question 2: Answer

The Nazis published posters like Source A to persuade women that their place was in the home. Many women would have accepted this and have been proud to serve Germany by raising children. Others, though, would have been unhappy with this role.

Under the Weimar Republic women had enjoyed a lot of freedom. They had jobs as teachers, civil servants and lawyers. They also enjoyed themselves going to night clubs etc. Now they were excluded from a lot of jobs and given a limited role. Many women would have needed persuading about the way the Nazis saw their role. So posters like this one were part of a propaganda campaign at the time devised to convince women that rearing children was their job.

Question 3: Answer

> I think that terror was more important. The Nazis had the SA and the SS who put a lot of fear into people. You would do as you were told if you thought that the SS was going to arrest you. There was also the Gestapo, or secret police, who spied on people. Fear is a good way of controlling people. The Nazis were crafty. Even the courts had Nazi judges. If you were accused of a crime you would not have much chance of getting off.
>
> The most feared things were the concentration camps. The first one was set up at Dachau in 1933. They were used to imprison anyone who criticised the government - Socialists, Communist etc. They were taken out of society and this made other people easier to control.

Question 1: Examiner's Comments on Answer

This is a thin answer, probably worth 3 marks. The student has made some reference to the poster and the opening sentence shows some background knowledge. There is, however, much more to say to get higher marks. Reference could be made to Source B and the significance of the person quoted. Mention could be made of how large families were encouraged (e.g. award of the Honour Cross of the German Mother) and how women were excluded from the professions. Mention could also be made of how the Nazis provided social welfare and child benefits.

Question 2: Examiner's Comments on Answer

A good answer. This student has seen that many women would have needed persuading to accept their lot under the Nazis. I like the way the student shows that the position of women under Weimar was freer but now they were being restricted. I give this 6 or 7 marks. Something could have been said about women having a political role under Weimar - another freedom now lost. Women had no place in Nazi politics!

Question 3: Examiner's Comments on Answer

This is not a bad answer. The student has picked one factor and explained it quite well. There is some good background knowledge. I would give it 4 or 5 marks. To get to the highest level with this sort of question it is necessary to consider both factors, explain them and show how both were part of the Nazi system. There are also many aspects of propaganda which could have been considered – the press, radio, posters, education, art and culture.

The Second World War

....1....

Topic Summary

In 1939 Germany invaded Poland and Hitler's popularity increased as German troops quickly overran Western Europe. By mid-1941, however, the military successes of earlier years began to dry up and opposition to the Fuhrer grew. Yet speaking out against Hitler's policies still required enormous courage and was an extremely dangerous thing to do.

....2....

What do I Need to Know?

You will need to know about the groups which opposed Hitler, even before the outbreak of war, and why their opposition was not effective. You will also have to be able to give details of growing opposition to the Nazis after 1941 and how that opposition was controlled.

Impact of the War, 1939–45
German civilians

- At first the German army won sweeping victories using blitzkrieg tactics. German civilians were shown propaganda films of the German army overrunning most of Western Europe. Most civilians were enthusiastic about the war at this stage.
- In 1941 Hitler invaded the Soviet Union. From this point, the civilians began to suffer hardship. The German army started to suffer setbacks. By 1942–3 German forces were being driven out of the Soviet Union and North Africa.
- German factories had to work long hours to produce arms. Food rationing meant that people had to live on a meagre diet.
- In 1943 Goebbels ran a propaganda campaign to boost the sagging morale of the civilians, claiming that victory was near.
- From 1943 German cities had to suffer constant bombing from the Allies. Gradually, many German people began to grow weary of the fighting and opposition to Hitler started to mount. He was seen less and less in public.

The Holocaust

- Hitler's early success meant he had the perfect chance to destroy the Jewish race.
- The 'Final Solution to the Jewish problem' was drawn up in 1942. It involved killing all Jewish people under German occupation:
  - Four special SS units (*Einsatzgruppen*) were used to murder Jews in the Soviet Union. By 1942, these units had killed 1,500,000 Jews.
  - Extermination camps were set up. Jews were transported to the camps and systematically gassed to death.
- Altogether 6 million Jews were murdered by the Nazis in what is now known as the Holocaust.

Resistance to Hitler and the Nazis

The period 1933–9

Despite the threat of the SS and Gestapo many groups spoke out against Hitler. Opponents of the Nazis needed great courage.

- The Social Democratic Party and the Communist Party both published anti-Nazi propaganda. Their opposition might have had more effect if they had joined forces, but the two groups did not trust each other.
- Church leaders, such as Martin Niemoller, criticised the regime and were imprisoned for their trouble.
- Many young people resented being indoctrinated and did not like the militarism of the Nazis. Some joined gangs such as the Edelweiss Pirates. They attacked members of the Nazi Youth.
- Some army generals, such as General Ludwig Beck, thought Hitler would get Germany into a war which it could not win. In 1938 Hitler sacked or forced the resignation of a number of generals to make sure he had the total obedience of the army.

The period 1939–45

When the war started to go badly for Germany there were some attempts to overthrow the regime.

- A group of Munich students called the White Rose printed anti-Nazi pamphlets. They appealed to people to follow a policy of passive resistance to the Nazis.
- The Church continued to speak out. Count Galen, the Catholic Bishop of Munster, criticised Hitler in his sermons. Dietrich Bonhoeffer, a Protestant minister, plotted against the Nazis. He was executed in 1945.
- Jews, forced to live in ghettos, rose up in armed revolt against the Nazis. The most famous rising took place in the Warsaw ghetto on 19 April 1943. There was also an uprising in the Treblinka death camp.
- A group of upper-class people, who called themselves the Kreisau Circle, believed Germany was being destroyed by Hitler. Many members of this group were executed in 1944–5.
- An attempt on Hitler's life was made in the July Plot 1944. The bomb went off but Hitler escaped.

Summary box 1

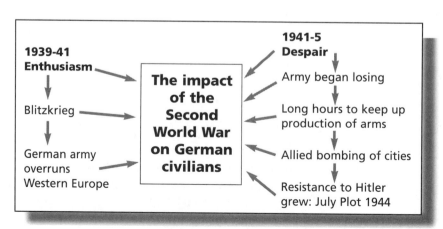

Summary box 2

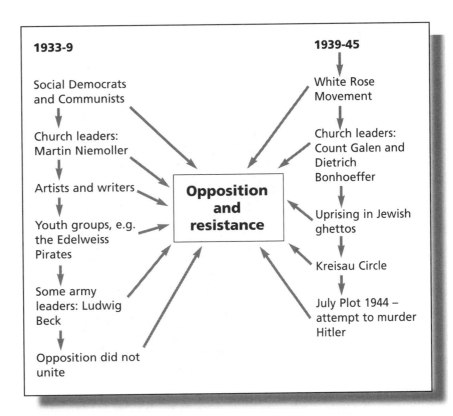

1933-9

Social Democrats and Communists
↓
Church leaders: Martin Niemoller
↓
Artists and writers
↓
Youth groups, e.g. the Edelweiss Pirates
↓
Some army leaders: Ludwig Beck
↓
Opposition did not unite

Opposition and resistance

1939-45

White Rose Movement

Church leaders: Count Galen and Dietrich Bonhoeffer
↓
Uprising in Jewish ghettos

Kreisau Circle

July Plot 1944 – attempt to murder Hitler

What do I Know?

Once you have revised this topic thoroughly you should be able to answer most of these questions without using your notes. How many can you get right?

Explain the importance of the following in the history of Germany:

- Night of the Long Knives
- The SS and Gestapo
- The German Labour Front
- The German economy
- Opposition to Hitler.

1 What tactic brought early success for Germany in 1939?
2 Where did Germany invade in 1941?
3 Why did the morale of German civilians drop after 1943?
4 What were *Einsatsgruppen*?
5 How many Jewish people were murdered by the Nazis?
6 Who were the 'Eidelweiss Pirates'?
7 What happened to Dietrich Bonhoeffer?
8 Why was opposition to Hitler not effective in the period 1933-9?
9 How did this opposition in the period 1933-9 differ from that before the war?
10 What happened in the July Plot of 1944?

My score........

4

Using the Sources

Study the sources and answer the questions to show that you understand the power of Hitler and his hold over the German people.

Source A

Ein Volk, ein Reich, ein Führer!

◀ A poster of Hitler. The slogan says 'One People, one Empire, one Leader.'

Source B

'I did not hear one word of criticism or disapproval of Hitler.'

▲ A comment in 1936 by David Lloyd George, a former British Prime Minister, after visiting Germany.

1 How popular was Hitler in the period 1933–45?

(**15 marks**)

2 Why were the Jews treated so badly in Nazi Germany?

(**10 marks**)

3 Was Hitler's dislike of Jews the only reason why they were persecuted? Explain your answer. (**10 marks**)

Hints for success

- In question 1 you should refer to the fact that in the 1930s many people thought that Germany needed a strong ruler to deal with the Depression and reverse the Treaty of Versailles. There were many problems to solve, but also some opposition. During the war opposition grew.
- In question 2 show how some German people distrusted the Jews (a mentality that went back a long time), and how others were affected by anti-Jewish propaganda. Provide supporting knowledge, e.g. the types of propaganda used. Also show how Hitler used them as a scapegoat to gain support.